GROUND BREAKING GUYS

40 MEN WHO BECAME GREAT BY DOING GOOD

STEPHANIE TRUE PETERS

ILLUSTRATED BY SHAMEL WASHINGTON

LITTLE, BROWN AND COMPANY
New York Boston

Little, Brown and Company
Hachette Book Group
1290 Avenue of the Americas, New York, NY 10104
Visit us at LBYR.com

First Edition: June 2019

Little, Brown and Company is a division of Hachette Book Group, Inc.
The Little, Brown name and logo are trademarks of Hachette Book Group, Inc.

The publisher is not responsible for websites (or their content) that are not owned by the publisher.

Library of Congress Cataloging-in-Publication Data
Names: Peters, Stephanie True, 1965– author. | Washington, Shamel, illustrator.
Title: Groundbreaking guys : 40 men who became great by doing good / by Stephanie True Peters ;
illustrated by Shamel Washington.
Other titles: Groundbreaking guys : forty men who became great by doing good
Description: First edition. | New York : Little, Brown and Company, 2019. | Audience: Ages 8-12.
Identifiers: LCCN 2018053959| ISBN 9780316529419 (hardcover) | ISBN 9780316529372 (ebook) |
ISBN 9780316529389 (library edition ebook)
Subjects: LCSH: Men—Biography. | Artists—Biography. | Celebrities—Biography. | Heroes—Biography.
Classification: LCC CT105 . P43 2019 | DDC 920.71—dc23
LC record available at https://lccn.loc.gov/2018053959

ISBNs: 978-0-316-52941-9 (hardcover), 978-0-316-52937-2 (ebook)

PRINTED IN CHINA

APS

10 9 8 7 6 5 4 3 2 1

About This Book
The illustrations for this book were rendered digitally. This book was edited by Farrin Jacobs and Anna Prendella
and designed by Karina Granda. The production was supervised by Virginia Lawther, and the production
editor was Andy Ball. The text was set in Avenir, and the display type is Goldana.

CONTENTS

INTRODUCTION 1

JOHN STUART MILL 2

ROBERT SMALLS 4

LOUIS BRANDEIS 6

DALIP SINGH SAUND 8

FENG-SHAN HO 10

ALAN TURING 12

JONAS SALK 14

JAMES BALDWIN 16

THÍCH NHẤT HẠNH 18

CESAR CHAVEZ 20

FRED ROGERS 22

MAURICE SENDAK 24

HARVEY MILK 26

ROBERTO CLEMENTE 28

N. SCOTT MOMADAY 30

WALTER DEAN MYERS 32

PATRICK STEWART AND IAN MCKELLEN............. 34

MUHAMMAD YUNUS 36

CARLOS SLIM HELÚ 38

HAYAO MIYAZAKI 40

MUHAMMAD ALI 42

BOB ROSS 44

STEVEN SPIELBERG 46

FREDDIE MERCURY 48

KAREEM ABDUL-JABBAR.............50

RANDY SHILTS 52

KAILASH SATYARTHI 54

WILLIAM HENRY "BILL" GATES.........56

ANTHONY BOURDAIN 58

JOHN BENNETT HERRINGTON............60

GEORGE CLOONEY 62

BARACK HUSSEIN OBAMA...........64

YO-YO MA 66

KYLAR W. BROADUS 68

TERRY CREWS 70

ZIAUDDIN YOUSAFZAI 72

QUESTLOVE 74

LIN-MANUEL MIRANDA 76

KENDRICK LAMAR................78

SOURCE NOTES 81

INTRODUCTION

What does it mean to be groundbreaking?

Our world has seen many incredible innovators, pioneers of all genders who made a difference with their inventions, thoughts, and actions. History books are full of men who have made their mark: rulers who shifted the course of a nation, explorers who traveled to new lands, and inventors, businessmen, philosophers, and soldiers who are remembered for their greatness. But these great men were not always *good* men.

The men you'll meet in this book come from different countries, have varying worldviews, and have excelled in a range of fields. They include scientists, like Jonas Salk, and playwrights, like Lin-Manuel Miranda. They come from countries including Japan, Bangladesh, and Mexico. While they might not always seem to have a lot in common, they share important qualities: These men served their communities. They treated people with respect. They lifted up others. They chose to listen and to care, even when doing so meant giving up control or feeling nervous or standing out. And these men went on to be groundbreaking, inspiring others and, indeed, doing great things—not in spite of their goodness but because of it.

Throughout history, it has been easier for some men to have power. Other people were locked out from power and oppressed—maybe no one respected them or cared about their communities or thought they were worth listening to. But they found a way to be heard. Power comes from a lot of places: you can make a difference because you make art, like Bob Ross, because you fight for human rights, like Dalip Singh Saund, because you speak out, like Terry Crews, or because you touch people's hearts, like Freddie Mercury. The men in this book all used whatever power they had to do good. They made it their mission to break new ground by putting good into the world, by connecting with other people and helping them.

And they were groundbreaking *as men*, because they changed the rules about what a man could be. They were unafraid to be gentle, to admit they were wrong, or to think outside the box. Their masculinity found new roots in compassion and consideration.

And you can do that, too. No matter what you're good at, or what makes you happy, these men prove that there are always ways to bring your talent and your strength to the world to make it better. You can make people feel better; you can make people's lives better. By being creative, kind, and honest, and by paying attention to the world around you, you can do better than great: you can do good.

JOHN STUART MILL

May 20, 1806–May 8, 1873

"Bad men need nothing more to compass their ends, than that good men should look on and do nothing."

Philosopher, political economist, colonial administrator, author, scholar: John Stuart Mill wore many hats during his lifetime. Born just outside London, England, Mill was only three years old when his domineering father, James, set him on a rigorous course of study that included Greek, Latin, world history, economics, and mathematics. In later years, John also studied with his father's friend, the philosopher Jeremy Bentham. Both Bentham and Mill's father believed in the philosophic doctrine of utilitarianism, which basically states that right actions, as opposed to wrong, are the ones that bring the most happiness to the greatest number. For example, utilitarianism argued that removing cruel or violent people from society would be morally right, because all other people would be happier.

Mill adopted this doctrine, too, but in his early twenties, he began to look at it in a new way. The change in his point of view came shortly after he had a nervous breakdown. While recuperating, he read the poetry of William Wordsworth and other Romantics. Their writings about humanity, nature, and creativity soothed his troubled spirit. They also led him to his new view of utilitarianism: if all individuals had more rights and freedoms, they would be happier, and therefore they would be better, and therefore society would be improved.

Mill wrote several books tying his brand of utilitarianism to political, judicial, economic, and social practices. His book *On Liberty* outlines the need for individuals to have creative and intellectual freedom—interestingly, something that his own education lacked. He wrote that colonialism and slavery, examples of what he called the "tyranny of the majority," should be abolished. Another of his books, *The Subjection of Women*, published in 1869, argued for greater rights for women, including the right to vote. It was a stance few men in his day took, and one he continued to hold after he was elected to Parliament.

Although such views are accepted as the norm in much of the modern world, in Mill's time they were radical. He proved the importance of deeply considering your own beliefs and being unafraid to hold on to them, even when they are unpopular. Today he is considered one of the most influential thinkers in social reform and liberalism.

nows only his own side of the case knows l

elf whether   nd you cease

rned   ing m

an u

nay caus   ly by his a

on, and in   justly accou

the injury.

f order or st   party of prog

necessary   a state of

w now   rks the

ROBERT SMALLS

April 5, 1839–February 23, 1915

"My race needs no special defense.... All they need is an equal chance in the battle of life."

Robert Smalls was born into slavery on a plantation in South Carolina. His mother, Lydia, worked in the plantation house, where she advocated for her teenage son to be sent to work in Charleston instead of in the fields.

In the 1850s, Charleston was a bustling port city. As an enslaved man, Smalls was sent to work on a steamer named the *Planter*, with pay sent back to the plantation slave owner. By age nineteen, he was the ship's unofficial pilot. Smalls was still with the *Planter* in 1860, when South Carolina seceded from the Union. He was also aboard it in April 1861, when the nearby stronghold of Fort Sumter fell to the Confederate Army in the epic battle that sparked the Civil War. The Confederates' takeover of Fort Sumter led US Navy ships to blockade Charleston Harbor.

This offered Robert Smalls a magnificent opportunity.

On the night of May 12, 1862, the soldiers stationed aboard the *Planter*, now a Confederate transport vessel, went ashore, leaving the ship attended only by enslaved crewmen. Smalls and eight others took control of the vessel. They sailed north, up the coast, where they picked up more slaves, including Smalls's wife and children. Disguised as soldiers, they steered the *Planter* past other Confederate ships, whose crews didn't look twice at the familiar vessel. As they drew alongside the Union blockade, Smalls hoisted the white flag of surrender. "Good morning, sir!" Smalls is said to have yelled to a crewman. "I've brought you some of the old United States guns, sir!"

The Union ship *Onward* took them on board...and Smalls, and every other person on his ship, were slaves no more. He had sailed them all to freedom.

In the days and months that followed, Smalls passed along vital information about the Charleston Harbor and the Confederate forces stationed there—information that enabled the Union to tighten its blockade of Charleston. He recruited thousands of black soldiers to join the Union fight. When the war ended, Smalls returned to his former master's home—and bought it.

If all that was not enough, in the 1870s and 1880s, Smalls served in the South Carolina state legislature and in the US House of Representatives. He introduced and championed revolutionary civil rights legislation, especially on voting and integration for black Americans. As when he sailed for freedom, it was not enough for Robert Smalls alone to succeed: he was going to take everyone else up with him.

LOUIS BRANDEIS

November 13, 1856–October 5, 1941

"If we desire respect for the law, we must first make the law respectable."

In 1908, a progressive lawyer named Louis Brandeis stood before the United States Supreme Court and argued in favor of regulating the wages and hours worked by women in the state of Oregon. To add weight to his case, he gave the justices a thoroughly researched legal brief containing expert testimony, social research, and references to factual sources and statistics about the problems these women would likely face without such regulation. When Brandeis won the case, his "Brandeis Brief," as that type of document would later be known, opened the door for future expert and statistical findings, such as that used in the landmark Supreme Court case *Brown v. Board of Education*, which overturned the legalized segregation of black and white students in public schools.

The son of liberal Jewish immigrants, Brandeis was raised to respect the rights of the individual. At age eighteen, he enrolled in Harvard Law School—despite not having a college degree. A star student, he graduated at the top of his class, with the highest grade point average to be achieved at the school for the next eighty years.

Nicknamed the "people's lawyer" and the "Robin Hood of the law," Brandeis often worked pro bono, meaning he refused payment, on cases concerning social injustice. He sought greater protections for working-class men and women and fought against the power and reach of big corporations, banks, and business monopolies. His book *Other People's Money and How the Bankers Use It* condemned the banking industry's practice of investing in schemes that made the wealthy even wealthier at the expense of those who were less fortunate. In his most famous article, "The Right to Privacy" (coauthored with fellow attorney Samuel D. Warren), he delivered a heartfelt and deftly written defense of the individual's "right to be let alone."

In 1916, President Woodrow Wilson appointed Brandeis to the Supreme Court. There, Brandeis supported distributing power through the states over allowing it to accumulate with the federal government, and shaped legal decisions that protected freedom of speech and personal privacy. Today Brandeis's progressive legacy lives on at the Massachusetts university that bears his name and in the laws and public policies he championed.

DALIP SINGH SAUND

September 20, 1899–April 22, 1973

"I don't care what a man has on top of his head. All I'm interested in is what he's got inside of it."

When Dalip Singh Saund was a graduate student in the early 1920s, he gave an impassioned talk calling for India's independence from Great Britain. Because he grew up in the Indian province of Punjab, Saund was confident in his argument—until a professor began lobbing questions that he couldn't answer. Saund learned a valuable lesson: If you're going to speak out, be prepared with the facts. You'll need them.

That lesson served him well years later when he entered politics. A successful farmer with a PhD in mathematics and a lifelong admiration for Abraham Lincoln, Saund was elected as a California county judge in 1952, a mere three years after he'd become a United States citizen. He was not able to vote until 1949, but he had always been tapped into political issues and had played a key role in garnering support for the Luce-Celler Act of 1946, the bill that opened the door to American citizenship for him and other Indian immigrants.

In 1956, Saund ran as a Democrat for an open congressional seat, speaking to the issues facing his district's farmers and business owners. And he won. Saund took 52 percent of the vote to become the first Sikh American, first Asian American, and first Indian American to sit in the House of Representatives. He won reelection in 1958 and 1960, too.

Throughout his career, Saund was a tireless supporter of the growing civil rights movement. He used his own story to add power to his speeches: "Ten years ago, I was not only a foreigner, I was an alien," he said in an address to Congress, "and today I have the honor to sit with the most powerful body of men on the face of the earth."

Saund believed that human rights should be supported internationally as well. "We have been coddling kings and dictators," he said, "and we then wonder why the poor people of the underdeveloped areas of the world do not appreciate the help of Uncle Sam." Many people didn't like hearing that, but Saund had the facts to back it up. He worked forcefully to ensure that the 1961 Foreign Assistance Act would limit or forbid aid to countries violating human rights.

Saund suffered a stroke in 1962 that limited his future work, but he had already made a great impact in bettering his country and helping others. As a role model, and as a pivotal figure in the American government's attention to civil rights at home and around the world, his legacy remains.

FENG-SHAN HO

September 10, 1901–September 28, 1997

"Seeing the Jews so doomed, it was only natural to feel deep compassion, and from a humanitarian standpoint, to be impelled to help them."

In March of 1938, over a year before World War II began, Adolf Hitler annexed Austria in his ongoing quest for world domination. Most Jewish Austrians were trapped unless they could produce a valid visa granting them entrance into another country. The international community, still reeling from World War I and not wanting to provoke animosity with Germany, chose not to intervene by force.

Less than eight months later, organized Nazi rioters stormed through the streets of Vienna. They destroyed Jewish-owned businesses, synagogues, and homes and attacked Jewish people in the streets, injuring some, killing others, and throwing thousands more into concentration camps. This night of terror became known as "Night of Broken Glass," or *Kristallnacht*. Witnessing the peril of the Austrian Jews, other nations expressed concern, even outrage, but did nothing to help.

Behind the scenes in Vienna, however, one Chinese diplomat had begun quietly assisting the Jews. Feng-Shan Ho was the Chinese consul general in Vienna. Horrified by the destruction and death he saw, he disobeyed direct orders from his superiors concerning Jewish immigrants and began issuing visas allowing entrance at Shanghai.

At that time China didn't require visas for entrance into Shanghai. But the documents Ho signed—twelve hundred in the first three months, and possibly thousands more in the months that followed—weren't about sending people to his homeland. The visas were about getting them safely out of Austria. Thanks to Ho's quiet defiance, hundreds, and possibly thousands, of innocent lives were saved.

Amazingly, no one knew the full extent of Ho's actions until after his death, when his daughter began digging into his past. She was dumbfounded to learn *how many* people he'd helped—but not by the fact that he'd helped them. "I was often asked why a Chinese diplomat would save Jews in Austria when others would not," she said. "My response has been, if you knew my father, you wouldn't have to ask."

In honor of his humanitarian efforts on behalf of Jews, Ho was posthumously awarded the title of Righteous Among the Nations by the World Holocaust Remembrance Center in Israel—one of only two Chinese individuals to be so named.

ALAN TURING

June 23, 1912–June 7, 1954

"Sometimes it is the people no one imagines anything of that do what no one can imagine."

On September 3, 1939, the United Kingdom declared war on Nazi Germany. The next day, the brilliant British mathematician, logician, and cryptographer Alan Turing joined a hush-hush wartime organization, the Government Code and Cypher School, headquartered at Bletchley Park, in Buckinghamshire, England.

At Bletchley Park, Turing designed an electro-mechanical decryption device known as a *bombe*. The bombe used cribs, or plaintext guesses, of the Nazis' encrypted text, to decipher messages sent by Hitler and his commanders via Enigma, a system of encryption machines. Thanks to Turing's ingenious approach, the Allied forces gained critical knowledge that helped them thwart Germany's efforts—ending World War II as much as two years sooner than it otherwise might have taken.

Turing's work at Bletchley Park was not his only secret, however. Turing was gay, and in those days same-sex relationships were illegal in England. In 1952, Turing's partner disclosed their relationship to the police while reporting a burglary, and both men were arrested and convicted of "gross indecency," a charge used to arrest men when it was discovered that they were gay. Rather than go to prison, Turing chose to receive a year of hormone injections, sometimes known as "chemical castration," meant to "correct" his sexuality. This discrimination and violence changed the course of his life.

Because of the conviction, Turing could no longer be part of the government's code-breaking program. But in the years that followed, Turing continued to work on a variety of scientific and academic projects, including research into plant biology and artificial intelligence. He is known as the father of theoretical computer science for his remarkable leaps in conceiving the future of computer programs. He invented the Turing test, which suggests that someday it will be possible for a computer to be indistinguishable from a human.

Turing died too young, and for seventy years, no one knew what he had done to help end the war. It wasn't until Queen Elizabeth II pardoned him in 2013—nearly sixty years after his death—that the public learned just how much they owed to his brilliance: how astonishing it was that a man with so much to lose would still risk everything to help his country win a war.

JONAS SALK

October 28, 1914–June 23, 1995

"Hope lies in dreams, in imagination, and in the courage of those who dare to make dreams into reality."

In the early 1900s, poliomyelitis, or polio, as the debilitating disease is more commonly known, left hundreds of thousands in the United States disabled with inadequate support, dying, or dead. Many of polio's victims were children. Polio had been around for centuries, yet scientists and medical doctors were still perplexed by the illness that would start with aches and a simple fever and would often render survivors paralyzed or on life support.

By the mid-1940s, medical researchers had discovered how the polio virus was transmitted. Now all they needed was a vaccine.

Enter Dr. Jonas Salk. Born in New York City, Salk had survived the polio outbreaks that had claimed the lives of so many during his childhood. He was the first in his family to attend college, and in 1939, he obtained his medical degree. Salk pursued a career in medical research. He studied influenza viruses and helped develop vaccines against them. In 1947, he switched to polio research. Within three years, he and his team were on the way to creating a vaccine to eradicate the disease, but they weren't fast enough to prevent an epidemic that claimed the lives of more than 3,000 people in the summer of 1952.

By 1955, however, Salk's vaccine was ready. Its effect on the world's population was nothing short of miraculous. Within ten years, the number of polio cases in the United States dropped to fewer than 1,000—and since its introduction to the world's population, the vaccine and subsequent supplemental vaccines have come close to wiping out the merciless disease completely.

In a decision just as lifesaving as his invention, Salk chose not to patent his vaccine, saying, "Could you patent the sun?" He knew that doing so would limit production, amid rampant demand, to the point where the vaccine would become unaffordable and people in poverty would continue to die.

Salk's contributions to medical science didn't end with the polio vaccine. In 1963, he founded the Salk Center for Biological Studies, where he and other scientists went on to study cancer, HIV/AIDS, and multiple sclerosis in the hope of discovering another miracle cure. While such breakthroughs have eluded scientists at the center so far, Salk himself once said, "We cannot be certain what will happen here, but we can be certain it will contribute to the welfare and understanding of man."

JAMES BALDWIN

August 2, 1924–December 1, 1987

"Not everything that is faced can be changed. But nothing can be changed until it is faced."

The author James Baldwin showed a knack for writing by the time he was nine years old. He composed the song for his school, PS 24 in Harlem, New York City, and wrote a play that the school performed. In his teens, Baldwin delivered sermons from the pulpit at the Pentecostal church where his stepfather preached, and he published stories and essays in his high school magazine. While he'd hoped to pursue writing in college, as the eldest of nine children, he had to help support his family instead.

But James didn't stop writing. He had too much to say, especially about the violent racism he witnessed and endured. His books delved deeply into the horrors of racism, and how they could be ended. Baldwin shed the same light on the harm that gay and bisexual men were dealt. Baldwin realized he was gay when he was a teenager but kept his sexuality private for years. In his thirties, he published his second novel, *Giovanni's Room*, which beautifully portrayed gay identities and relationships. The book stunned readers. When asked years later why he'd risked his career, he responded: "If I hadn't written that book, I would have had to stop writing altogether."

Baldwin moved to Paris when he was twenty-four to escape America's racism. But after the 1963 publication of *The Fire Next Time*, a nonfiction book that spoke of the need for white Americans to truly empathize with black Americans, he frequently returned to the United States to give lectures and meet with influential people who shared his concerns about racial inequality.

One such meeting, in May of 1963, was with Robert F. Kennedy, the brother of and attorney general to President John F. Kennedy. Baldwin spelled out why the administration needed to do better by the civil rights movement: "Your family has been here for three generations and your brother's on top. My family has been here a lot longer than that and we're still on the bottom. That is the heart of the problem."

It takes every kind of fighter and helper to build a movement, and Baldwin's precise, forthright explanations of how prejudice worked played a crucial role in opening people's eyes all around the world—and calling them to the tasks at hand.

THÍCH NHẤT HẠNH

October 11, 1926–

"Our own life has to be our message."

Zen master and Buddhist monk Thích Nhất Hạnh is an author, poet, and peace activist, as well as the founder of Engaged Buddhism, a movement that pairs the concept of mindfulness—living in the present moment—with peaceful activism. Above all, Thích Nhất Hạnh is a teacher.

Nhất Hạnh was drawn to Buddhism after seeing a tranquil picture of the Buddha in a magazine when he was seven years old. When he was sixteen, he entered a Buddhist monastery in Vietnam. He was ordained as a monk seven years later, and shortly after that, he moved to the United States, where he taught religion at Princeton and Columbia Universities before returning to Vietnam in 1963.

His homeland was in the grip of the Vietnam War. Their torn country was invaded by soldiers from multiple countries, including the United States. Many monks chose to withdraw from the turmoil and focus on their meditative practices. Nhất Hạnh continued his studies, but didn't confine himself within the monastery's walls. Instead, he sought ways to bring peace to his country.

He established the Order of Interbeing, a group of Buddhists who strove to replace hatred and violence with compassion and mindfulness. He trained the School for Youth and Social Service to rebuild war-torn communities and improve access to education and health care. He founded a book publishing company and a magazine dedicated to spreading the ideals of Buddhism. And he traveled to other nations to advocate for a peaceful resolution to the war. Dr. Martin Luther King Jr., who met Nhất Hạnh in 1966, was so impressed by the monk that he nominated Nhất Hạnh for the 1967 Nobel Peace Prize. "His ideas for peace," King stated in his letter to the Nobel committee, "would build a monument to…world brotherhood, to humanity."

Today, Nhất Hạnh shares his message of peace from Plum Village, a Buddhist community he founded in southern France. He recently started Wake Up, an international program for young adults who want to create a more compassionate global society. Through the Thích Nhất Hạnh Foundation, he and his followers bring solace and aid to underserved communities.

And he does it all with a warm smile, for, as he once said, "A smile is the most basic kind of peace work."

CESAR CHAVEZ

March 31, 1927–April 23, 1993

"Ours is a revolution of the mind and heart."

As a teenager, Cesar Chavez lived under conditions he would later fight to change. When he was a child, he and his family moved from Arizona to California, after dishonest men had swindled them out of their home. His family took jobs as migrant farmworkers, following the harvests up and down California. It was grueling work, made worse by miserable living conditions, racism, corruption, and paltry wages.

Exposing and changing this exploitation became Chavez's life mission. After two years in the US Navy, he returned to California, later joining the Community Service Organization, a group dedicated to Latino civil rights that had taken a keen interest in giving migrant workers a voice. Chavez rose through the ranks to become the national director, but when his push to organize the farmworkers was rejected, he moved on and cofounded the National Farm Workers Association with fellow activist Dolores Huerta.

Beneath its distinctive black, red, and white Aztec eagle flag, the NFWA, later called the United Farm Workers, fought to raise awareness of the indignities suffered by its workers. "Generation after generation have sought to demoralize us, to break our human spirit," Chavez once wrote.

Chavez had quit school early—he didn't go beyond seventh grade—but when he wasn't working, he spent his time reading and learning. The teachings of Indian leader Mahatma Gandhi, who believed in nonviolent resistance, intrigued him. Though the ongoing injustice angered him, Chavez fought back with nonviolent actions: strikes, walkouts, marches, and boycotts. In 1965, he and the NFWA used these tactics to protest the unjust treatment of migrant grape farmworkers of Delano, California. It took five years, but the workers emerged with better pay, benefits, and protections. Chavez often took the burden of dissent on himself. In 1988, he went without food for thirty-six days to protest the use of pesticides in the grape industry, which he called "systemic poisoning."

Chavez passed away in 1993; his fight for the rights of the Latino and labor communities continues through the Cesar Chavez Foundation. The year after his death, he was posthumously awarded the Presidential Medal of Freedom by President Bill Clinton in recognition of his lifelong commitment to the migrant workers.

¡Sí, se puede!

FRED ROGERS

March 20, 1928–February 27, 2003

"It takes strength to talk about our feelings and to reach out for help and comfort when we need it."

From February 19, 1968, to August 31, 2001, a soft-spoken man named Fred Rogers sang an invitation to young television viewers at home every weekday: "Won't you be my neighbor?" He and his show, *Mister Rogers' Neighborhood*, are iconic: his red zippered cardigan and blue canvas sneakers make neighbors around the world feel seen, welcomed, and loved—just for being themselves.

Singer, songwriter, musician, puppeteer: Fred McFeely Rogers's talents were a good match for children's television. So was his education in theology and child development, as well as his personal belief that to become caring, thoughtful adults, children needed to understand their own feelings. They needed to know that their feelings mattered—that they *themselves* mattered. This wasn't something that many people said to children back then. Fred Rogers changed that.

With a cast of puppets he voiced, a real-life community of neighbors, and kid-friendly activities, Rogers gave his audience a safe place to explore their emotions. Anger, frustration, grief, joy: he addressed them all openly and patiently.

In 1969, the United States government considered slashing the budget for the Corporation for Public Broadcasting and its educational programming. Rogers appeared before a Senate subcommittee and calmly explained why his show was important.

"I give an expression of care every day to each child," he told Senator John Pastore on behalf of public broadcast programs. "A meaningful expression of care." He ended his testimony with lyrics to one of his songs: "And what a good feeling to feel like this! And to know that the feeling is really mine."

Pastore, dismissive of Rogers at first, admitted he got goose bumps then. "Looks like you just earned the twenty million dollars," he said. It was twice the amount previously allotted to public broadcasting.

Rogers's message lives on in every child he spoke to. A postage stamp with his image was issued in 2018, the fiftieth anniversary of the debut of his show. March 20, Fred Rogers's birthday, is national "Won't You Wear a Sweater Day." Somewhere in space is an asteroid bearing his name—26858 Misterrogers. And in a special case at the Smithsonian's National Museum of American History in Washington, DC, is a certain red zippered cardigan!

MAURICE SENDAK

June 10, 1928–May 8, 2012

"Let the wild rumpus start!"

Legendary children's book author Maurice Sendak often credited his childhood illnesses for inspiring his creativity. Stuck in bed in his Brooklyn, New York, apartment, he let his imagination run wild. He had a talent for drawing and let his artwork take him to fantastic places. Many times, those places were scary—not surprising, since Sendak grew up through the Great Depression, World War II, and the Holocaust; many members of his Polish Jewish family were killed in Hitler's concentration camps.

Sendak continued making art in high school and worked part-time adding color to comic strips. But when he was twenty years old, helping build window displays for the famous New York toy store FAO Schwarz, the children's book buyer introduced him to an editor named Ursula Nordstrom.

Sendak began by illustrating books written by other people, then moved on to writing his own. The first of those, published in 1956, was *Kenny's Window*, about a lonely boy who dreams of faraway adventures. Seven years later, he published his most famous book: *Where the Wild Things Are*. The book captivated readers not only with its fantastical monsters and creepy forest but with its destructive, defiant main character, Max. Max struck a chord because, as Sendak once said, "We're animals. We're violent. We're criminal....You know, kids are hard." Not everyone liked that. People warned that children would be traumatized by the artwork or learn bad behaviors from Max. But in 1964, the book won the Caldecott Medal, the top prize in children's picture books.

Sendak went on to write and illustrate many other beloved children's books. He wasn't interested in telling children how to behave: he told strange, beautiful stories in which the grief and fear he felt as a child could be acknowledged and cared for. All his books explored this wildness in some shape or form, forever changing the landscape of children's literature by making space for children to have messy, difficult feelings—and to express those feelings.

Sendak, who was gay and lived with his partner for fifty years, challenged the silencing of both feelings and social oppression. His picture book *We Are All in the Dumps with Jack and Guy* shone a light on the HIV/AIDS crisis at its peak; in his books, he also explored isolation, poverty, and shame, even when people didn't want him to.

Later in life, he adapted many of his works for theater, television, opera, and ballet, reaching new audiences with his weirdly wonderful creations and courageous, unapologetically complicated characters.

HARVEY MILK

May 22, 1930–November 27, 1978

"We will not win our rights by staying quietly in our closet."

When Harvey Milk moved to San Francisco in 1972, he wasn't setting out to be one of the country's first openly gay politicians. He grew up in New York, where he had worked in insurance and finance research. But soon after moving into the Castro District, where much of the city's gay population lived, he became troubled by how law enforcement openly targeted gay and bisexual men, and by how big money influenced local politics. Hoping to create real, practicable changes, he ran for a spot on the city's Board of Supervisors. After a few early losses, he finally won a seat in late 1977.

"The Mayor of Castro Street," as Milk was called, was a well-known LGBT (lesbian, gay, bisexual, transgender) rights activist by then, in a time when LGBT people were often not accepted by their families and communities, and faced discrimination and violence throughout the United States. In 1974, he had founded the Castro Village Association, the first-ever group dedicated to bolstering gay-owned businesses. That same year, he had organized the inaugural Castro Street Fair, a daylong arts and entertainment celebration of the LGBT community that is still held today.

As a city supervisor, Milk scored big victories to make California's LGBT community safer. In April 1978, his measure, the San Francisco Gay Rights Ordinance, was approved by a vote of ten to one. "This one has teeth," Milk told reporters. "A person can go to court if his rights are violated." Later that same year, he helped defeat the Briggs Initiative, a mandate calling for the firing of California's gay public school teachers and administrators. A charismatic public speaker, Milk called for more gay leaders to come forward so that young people struggling with their sexuality could have strong, positive role models.

Not everyone appreciated his message. In fact, Milk received so many death threats that he predicted he would be assassinated one day. Sadly, that prediction came true. On November 27, 1978, a disgruntled former colleague cornered Milk in his office and fatally shot him.

Today, Milk is an icon of the LGBT community. In 2009, President Barack Obama recognized his contribution to gay rights by posthumously awarding him the Presidential Medal of Freedom. In his remarks, the president repeated Milk's own mantra: "You gotta give 'em hope."

ROBERTO CLEMENTE

August 18, 1934–December 31, 1972

"I want to be remembered as a ballplayer who gave all he had to give."

On New Year's Eve 1972, Pittsburgh Pirates right fielder Roberto Clemente boarded a chartered airplane bound for Managua, the capital of Nicaragua. The city had been hit by a devastating earthquake the week before. Clemente wanted to make sure the plane's relief supplies reached the victims—unlike three previous loads, which had been stolen by corrupt officials.

The new supplies didn't reach their destination, either. Just moments after takeoff, the overloaded plane crashed into the Atlantic Ocean off Puerto Rico. Everyone aboard perished.

Clemente's death shook players and fans. A superstar on the field, the Great One, as he was known, had won twelve Gold Glove awards and four National League batting titles and been named the NL's Most Valuable Player in 1966. He received the World Series Most Valuable Player Award in 1971 and was an All-Star for twelve seasons.

But Clemente's impact went far beyond the game. In an era rife with racism, Clemente, who was Puerto Rican, served as a role model for other Latin Americans, a responsibility he took on for himself, and took very seriously. It's astonishing that, although racism made Clemente's job more painful than it was for other baseball players, he was not content to merely do his job and reap its rewards, as many of them were: Clemente always focused on giving back and lifting others up. He observed, "What we needed was a Puerto Rican player…someone to look up to and try to equal."

In the off-season, Clemente did his best to be that someone. He played in winter leagues and held baseball clinics for children in Puerto Rico. He volunteered as manager to Puerto Rican amateur teams, and in fact had been with one such team in Nicaragua for a competition just before the earthquake struck. He typically was not outspoken, yet he was never shy about sharing his opinions on racism. "I believe that every human being is equal, but one has to fight hard all the time to maintain that equality," he once said.

Baseball honored Clemente by electing him to the Baseball Hall of Fame fewer than three months after his death, inducting him only six months later—a break with tradition, for players usually had to be retired for at least five years before even being considered. Today, his legacy lives on with the Roberto Clemente Award for community involvement, sportsmanship, and contributions to a player's team. And every September, fans and players celebrate Roberto Clemente Day in the Great One's memory.

N. SCOTT MOMADAY

February 27, 1934–

"A word has power in and of itself. It comes from nothing into sound and meaning; it gives origin to all things."

N. Scott Momaday once described his childhood as a "Pan-Indian experience." The Kiowa poet, writer, painter, and teacher moved with his parents from one southwestern reservation to another, from Navajo to Apache to Pueblo, often living without electricity or indoor plumbing. Many times, he would be the only student in his class who could speak English well. But each place he lived was always rich in tradition, and Momaday never tired of listening to his father and others retell the stories that the Kiowa and other Native Americans handed down through the generations.

Momaday wove those stories and his own experiences on the reservations into his writing, including his first novel, *House Made of Dawn*, which won the Pulitzer Prize for Fiction in 1969. This groundbreaking book inspired other Native people, whose writing pushed open the doors to the publishing world. This new wave of American Indian literature became widely known as the Native American Renaissance. The term was controversial: Many Native people rightfully pointed out that Native artists and creators had been creating successfully and beautifully for thousands of years. Others still thought it important to emphasize the fact that Native works had finally broken into a new sphere at a time of great oppression. Regardless, Momaday's pivotal writing was at the forefront of a sweeping movement of literary growth.

Momaday's impact has been felt in other ways as well. He has appeared in several documentaries about Native Americans and has lent his melodic voice to exhibits in the Smithsonian Institution's National Museum of the American Indian, of which he is a founding trustee. As a professor at the University of California at Berkeley, he developed new courses on Indian studies, oral traditions and mythology, and literature. He paints, using motifs and images from the Kiowa and other Native American tribes.

"I am lucky," Momaday once said, "because I do have a sense of my Indian heritage. That's very firmly fixed in my imagination and in my mind." Throughout all his varied pursuits as an artist and advocate, Momaday is ensuring that that heritage is valued and carried forward. He was awarded the National Medal of Arts in 2007, in recognition of his creative contributions "that celebrate and preserve Native American art and oral tradition."

WALTER DEAN MYERS

August 12, 1937–July 1, 2014

"Reading pushed me to discover worlds beyond my landscape."

Walter Milton Myers was just two years old when his mother died. He passed into the care of Herbert and Florence Dean—a name he later took as his middle name—and moved from the rural town of Martinsburg, West Virginia, to Harlem, New York. Florence taught Walter to read, as she had taught herself. Walter started with magazines and graduated to comic books, which he devoured until a teacher caught him with one during class. "She tore it up," he recalled. "I was really upset, but then she brought in a pile of books from her own library. That was the best thing that ever happened to me."

Later, at the advice of another teacher, he began trying his hand at writing. Even after he dropped out of high school and joined the army, he continued to write. When his military service ended, he found work writing magazine articles, marketing copy, short stories, and more. His big break came in 1968, when he entered a picture book manuscript, *Where Does the Day Go?*, in a contest run by the Council on Interracial Books for Children—and won. The book was published in 1969, and from then on, writing books was what he did.

Myers published more than one hundred award-winning and critically acclaimed books for children, ranging from picture books to young adult novels and even memoir, history, and poetry. His work shines a compassionate, nuanced spotlight on the experiences of young black people in America—stories that were missing from the books available to him as a child. Growing up, he'd read book after book about white children by white authors. Changing that silence was vital. He once wrote, "If we continue to make black children nonpersons by excluding them from books and by degrading the black experience, and if we continue to neglect white children by not exposing them to any aspect of other racial and ethnic experiences in a meaningful way, we will have a next racial crisis." His books were at the forefront of change for readers around the world—many of whom, inspired by him, would grow up to become writers.

In recognition of his lifelong contribution to the literary arts, the Library of Congress appointed Myers the National Ambassador for Young People's Literature. He was the first African American author to hold the title. From 2012 to 2013, he toured the country, promoting literacy and education.

Today, the organization We Need Diverse Books has an award specifically for celebrating great achievement in "diverse books by diverse authors." It is known as the Walter.

PATRICK STEWART AND IAN MCKELLEN

July 13, 1940–
May 25, 1939–

*"Violence is a choice a man makes
and he alone is responsible for it." –Patrick Stewart*

*"I've never met a gay person who regretted coming out–
including myself." –Ian McKellen*

British actors and pop culture icons Patrick Stewart and Ian McKellen became friends in 1999, when they co-starred in the movie *X-Men*. "Ian and I would talk for hours," recalled Stewart, "and found out how much we had in common."

While both are noted stage actors and have been knighted for their contributions to the dramatic arts, these best friends are also very involved in helping others. Stewart still remembers being a helpless child witnessing his father abusing his mother. He supports organizations that help victims of domestic violence. "Though not able to do something for my mother," he said, "I [am] doing something in her name, which would help women in a similar situation." Stewart also supports Combat Stress, which reaches out to veterans suffering from post-traumatic stress disorder and other afflictions—something he now believes his father, who served in World War II, likely suffered from.

McKellen, who is gay, came out in 1988—when it was not easy to be an out gay man—to fight against a homophobic law proposed in Great Britain. In 1989, he founded the LGBT rights group Stonewall, whose motto is Acceptance without Exception. McKellen proved wrong the belief that coming out ruined actors' careers with his culture-changing roles, including Magneto in *X-Men* and Gandalf in the Lord of the Rings trilogy. Of his own career, McKellen has said: "Nothing in life is more important to me than helping young people realize that there are better days ahead of them."

When their busy careers permit, the two unite to support each other with open affection, playfulness, and compassion. At a time when many men are still told they should not show those feelings, especially to other men, Stewart and McKellen are the happy proof of how wrong that belief is.

MUHAMMAD YUNUS

June 28, 1940–

"Poverty is a threat to peace."

"**W**hat is the point of all these splendid economic theories when people around me are dying of hunger?"

That was the question thirty-four-year-old Muhammad Yunus asked himself in 1974. He was back in his homeland of Bangladesh after years in the United States, where he had studied economics. Among the most basic economic principles was that banks lent people money, and in turn, those people repaid the loans to the banks with interest. In order not to lose money, the banks demanded that people offer something of value as collateral—a house, a car, land. Anyone who could not come up with collateral was denied a loan. Those denied most often? The poor. If they didn't have anything yet, they were stuck with nothing.

And, Yunus knew, the poor were the ones who were most in need of those loans. Without that money, they lacked the wherewithal to create products or build and grow businesses. Without those products or businesses, they couldn't earn money, and therefore stood little chance of ever climbing out of poverty. Their children would face the same fate—and so on through the generations. So Yunus decided that if existing banks would not give the poor money, he would create one that would.

Grameen Bank, Bank for the Poor, opened seven years later. Under Yunus's guidance, it began lending small amounts of seed money, sometimes as little as thirty dollars, to local craftsmen. Their successes spurred more lending, which led to growth, even more successes, and a cycle of upward financial mobility that boosted Bangladesh's overall economic standing.

Grameen Bank is also unique in that it lends money to both men *and* women, whereas some banks still refuse loans to women, especially when they live in poverty. Women who are financially independent are better equipped to pursue their own interests and goals, and drive their societies forward; financially stable mothers are better equipped to help care for and educate their children. And everyone had to agree that healthy, well-educated children meant a brighter future for Bangladesh.

In recognition for his humanitarian, out-of-the-box approach to his country's economic needs, Yunus and Grameen Bank were awarded the Nobel Peace Prize in 2006. "Poverty does not belong in a civilized human society," Yunus once wrote. "Its proper place is in a museum. That's where it will be."

CARLOS SLIM HELÚ

January 28, 1940–

"You will make mistakes many times....
Try to make them small, then accept, correct, and forget them."

When Carlos Slim Helú was a young boy, his father gave him a weekly allowance of five pesos (about twenty-five cents in today's US currency). Carlos recorded any purchases he made and their amount in a special ledger. He managed his money so well that by the time he was a teenager, he had enough to become a shareholder in a bank and invest in a mining company. By 2010, he was the wealthiest man in the world, a rank he held for the next three years.

Slim, as the self-made billionaire is known, uses his wealth to enrich the lives of others, because, as he once said, "Businessmen should participate in solving problems…doing, more than giving." His Fundación Carlos Slim supports education, health care, and the arts; its past endeavors include funding cataract surgeries in Peru, small-business development in Colombia, and computer training in Mexico. The foundation also backs the Museo Soumaya, a museum named for his late wife, Soumaya, filled with world-renowned paintings and sculpture, and where admission is free. The World Wildlife Fund is also a frequent recipient of funds from this foundation.

A second foundation, Fundación Telmex, helps grow Mexico's amateur sports programs, provides money for teaching and education initiatives, and develops humanitarian aid in response to natural disasters. And Fundación del Centro Histórico de la Ciudad de México, A.C., works to revitalize Mexico City's historic downtown area.

Slim is an avid supporter of sustainability and green energy. He has campaigned for better access to potable drinking water and waste-removal systems, as well as improved infrastructure throughout the world. He has urged the international business community to take a more active role in addressing climate change and human rights violations.

He does all this because he hopes to help future generations get off on the right foot. "Most people try to make a better world for our children," Slim once said, "when what they should be doing is making better children for our world."

HAYAO MIYAZAKI

January 5, 1941–

"You must see with eyes unclouded by hate."

Many activists bring attention to their causes with bold outward displays—protests, rallies, signs, speeches, and so forth. But others take a subtler approach and speak the truth through their stories. Hayao Miyazaki, master storyteller, anime director, and cofounder of the award-winning animation company Studio Ghibli, is one such person.

Quiet by nature, Miyazaki doesn't often publicly protest about the issues that trouble him, and in that respect, he doesn't fit the usual image of an activist. But as anyone who has seen his films knows, meaningful messages do not have to be shouted to be heard.

Miyazaki weaves environmental, pacifist, and feminist themes through his work. *Nausicaä of the Valley of the Wind*, *Princess Mononoke*, and *My Neighbor Totoro*—three of his best-known movies—all speak to the importance of protecting, respecting, and living harmoniously with nature. *Howl's Moving Castle* and *Princess Mononoke* demonstrate that conflict can be resolved through nonviolent means rather than through war and bloodshed. And through young female characters who discover their inner strength—Chihiro of *Spirited Away* and Sophie of *Howl's Moving Castle*, to name just two—girls find critical role models. His movies' ideas stay with people because they speak directly to the heart.

Miyazaki's childhood no doubt influenced his beliefs and his work. Born in Japan during World War II, he experienced the horrors of war firsthand when his hometown was heavily bombed and half of it was destroyed. Even though his family had moved six months earlier to the countryside near a forest not unlike the one featured in *My Neighbor Totoro*, the loss was inescapable. His father, an aeronautical engineer, worked on airplanes in the family factory. Miyazaki was fascinated by the craft, though he later admitted that part of him was disturbed that the machines were used for war. His mother was bedridden with spinal tuberculosis—and still ran the household efficiently and commandingly from her bed.

"I yearned for an earnest and pure world," Miyazaki once said. "I wanted to make something life affirming." As his legions of fans would agree, Miyazaki has accomplished just that—and maybe helped others realize that they can work for change in an infinite number of ways, including by sharing stories of compassion and kindness.

MUHAMMAD ALI

January 17, 1942–June 3, 2016

"If my mind can conceive it, and my heart can believe it– then I can achieve it."

In the world of professional boxing, no one is more famous than heavyweight champion Muhammad Ali. He started boxing when he was twelve years old, and in 1960 he won a gold medal at the Olympic Games. A trash-talking, fiercely proud athlete with lightning-quick punches, Ali went on to earn an impressive record of fifty-six wins—thirty-seven of which were won by knockout— out of a total of sixty-one bouts. But perhaps his most historic fight started with his refusal to fight.

By 1967, the United States had sent combat troops into Vietnam in a controversial war. Ali was drafted into the army. He refused to serve. "Man, I ain't got no quarrel with them Viet Cong," he told reporters. Ali was immediately convicted of draft evasion, stripped by boxing authorities of his championship titles and boxing license, and sentenced to five years in jail.

Ali fought the charges all the way to the Supreme Court, which ruled in his favor three and a half years later. During those years, he embraced a new role: spokesperson for the growing black pride and anti-war movements. At universities across the country he railed against America's deep culture of racism and its involvement in the Vietnam War. He also spoke about his conversion to Islam and the renunciation of his birth name, which he called his "slave name." Supporters hailed the charismatic athlete activist as a hero. Others loudly denounced him as unpatriotic, a coward, a draft dodger—and much worse. But Ali never wavered from his stances.

Ali returned to the boxing ring in 1970, where he delighted fans with his merciless taunts of his opponents and his hard-fought victories. Out of the ring, he followed his faith's edict to help those in need. He donated millions to feed the hungry, traveled the world on goodwill missions to war-torn and impoverished countries, and protested human and civil rights violations. He was awarded the Presidential Medal of Freedom for being "a fierce fighter and a man of peace."

Soon after he retired from boxing in 1981, Ali was diagnosed with Parkinson's, a disease that robs the victim of muscle control. The once powerful boxer shied away from the limelight—until the opening ceremonies of the 1996 Summer Olympics. There, the former Olympic gold medalist emerged from the shadows high above a packed stadium and, with shaking hands, proudly held the Olympic torch aloft for all to see.

BOB ROSS

October 29, 1942–July 4, 1995

"Anybody can paint.
All you need is a dream in your heart, a little practice."

Listening to the soft-spoken Bob Ross describe how to paint a happy little tree on his long-running PBS television show, you would never believe that he was in the military for twenty years. But if not for that, Ross might never have discovered painting. A native of Florida, Ross joined the air force at age eighteen. He was sent to Alaska, where he saw mountains and snow for the first time. He felt inspired to capture them on canvas. He took an art class, bought supplies, and started to paint what he saw. He himself acknowledged that his artwork wasn't high caliber, but to his surprise and delight, people wanted to buy it. Soon he was earning more money as a painter than as a sergeant.

When Ross was in the military, he had to yell a lot. The culture of the military was tough and strict, and for twenty years, Ross was surrounded by it. "I was the guy who makes you scrub the latrine, the guy who makes you make your bed, the guy who screams at you for being late to work," he once said. However, after he retired from the service, he chose never to raise his voice again. After years of yelling, Bob Ross wanted to be gentle.

After the military, Ross embarked on a new career as an art teacher. Money was tight until a local public television station in need of programming saw a tape his wife had made of him narrating his painting technique. The producers liked how Ross addressed the camera as if he were talking directly to a single person and appreciated that he could produce a complete painting in a short, filmable period of time. They decided to give him a shot. And with that, Ross's long-running show, *The Joy of Painting*, was born.

From 1983 until 1994, viewers tuned in to watch the man with the sky-high curls demonstrate how to turn a blank canvas into mountains, meadows, lakes, and forests—always with a bright-eyed kindness and encouragement. Ross told them that it didn't matter if they were talented; what mattered was that they had fun. Mistakes, he said, were just "happy accidents." Anyone could learn, and anyone was welcome.

STEVEN SPIELBERG

December 18, 1946–

"I don't dream at night. I dream at day, I dream all day, I'm dreaming for a living."

Steven Spielberg, the cinematic genius behind the blockbuster franchises Jaws, Indiana Jones, and Jurassic Park, as well as dozens of other standout movies, was bullied as a child. "I was a nerd in those days," he recalled.

But he was bullied for more than that. As his mother once told a reporter, he was also sometimes the target of cruel, even violent anti-Semitic bigotry. To protect himself, Spielberg said later, "I often told people my last name was German, not Jewish."

Spielberg protected himself in another way: by disappearing behind a movie camera. He soon discovered that making movies was something he enjoyed and something he was very, very good at. Years later, that moviemaking talent helped him confront the anti-Semitism he'd faced as a child.

In 1993, Spielberg released the movie *Schindler's List*, the true story of German businessman Oskar Schindler, who single-handedly saved the lives of more than a thousand Jewish people during World War II. During filming, Spielberg immersed himself in the Holocaust's horrific and highly personal history. That history continued to haunt him even after the movie wrapped because he knew that for far too many Jews, anti-Semitism wasn't history at all. The Jewish people were still victims of discrimination and hatred.

Spielberg wanted to change that. So, in 1994, he established what is now the USC Shoah Foundation to record survivor testimony. "Students connect with survivors through watching their testimony," he said. "And they take that with them into their lives." In 1995, he used his profits from *Schindler's List* to create the Righteous Persons Foundation, an organization that seeks to preserve Jewish history and bolster its present community by funding the arts and entrepreneurship. To date, RPF has donated $100 million in grants for worthy projects. Spielberg has proven himself committed to telling fantastic, life-changing stories—and to changing people's lives in reality, as well.

Spielberg once wondered of Oskar Schindler, "What would drive a man like this to suddenly take everything he had earned and put it all in the service of saving these lives?" With the Shoah Foundation, RPF, and the countless other charities he supports, he seems to have found his answer.

FREDDIE MERCURY

September 5, 1946–November 24, 1991

"I won't be a rock star. I will be a legend."

On April 20, 1992, 72,000 fans packed Wembley Stadium in London for a concert in tribute to a wildly popular singer, songwriter, and performer: Freddie Mercury of the rock band Queen.

Months earlier, Mercury had revealed that he was dying of HIV/AIDS, a little-understood disease with no cure. "I hope that everyone will join with me, my doctors, and all those worldwide in the fight against this terrible disease," he said. The next day, Mercury passed away. With the April Freddie Mercury Tribute Concert, his friends honored his request.

Freddie Mercury was born Farrokh "Freddie" Bulsara in Zanzibar (now Tanzania). He developed his love of music early, taking piano lessons when he was seven and forming a rock band, the Hectics, with classmates when he was twelve.

When he was seventeen, Bulsara and his family fled to the United Kingdom to escape war. He earned a degree in graphic design before returning to his true love: rock music. "I'm one of those people who believes in doing those things which interest you," he said. He joined the group Smile in 1971, and at his suggestion, Smile changed its name to Queen—and Bulsara changed his name to Freddie Mercury.

When performing with Queen, Mercury thrilled crowds as few ever have. His astonishing voice spanned four octaves, and his songwriting was pure gold. Ten of the seventeen songs on their *Greatest Hits* album were written and sung by Mercury, including "Bohemian Rhapsody," the band's best-known number. He brought all of his passion and energy to every electric performance, making every show a celebration, and making audiences feel like they were welcomed into something special. But offstage, he was a different person—quiet, shy, and private. Few people knew that he was bisexual.

For many people, Freddie Mercury first humanized the HIV/AIDS crisis. Speaking publicly about his condition was an act of bravery at the time, one he knew could help others long after he was gone. He had touched their hearts, and even after his passing, people wanted to give back. And they did. His bandmates and friends created the Mercury Phoenix Trust, a charitable organization that, since 1992, has received more than $15 million to be donated to AIDS research and assistance.

The initial funding came from the tribute concert. Queen's drummer, Roger Taylor, said that night: "It's to tell everybody around the world that AIDS affects us all….You can cry as much as you like."

KAREEM ABDUL-JABBAR

April 16, 1947–

"I can do more than stuff a ball through a hoop; my greatest asset is my mind."

During his twenty-year NBA career, basketball legend Kareem Abdul-Jabbar was famous for his untouchable skyhook—a shot made by lofting the ball high above and away from defenders and flicking it into the hoop. Today, the seven-foot-two-inch sports icon is known for another skyhook: his Skyhook Foundation and its mission to introduce underserved children to science, technology, engineering, and math, or STEM.

Abdul-Jabbar grew up in Harlem, where resident black artists and intellectuals—Louis Armstrong, Langston Hughes, and W. E. B. Du Bois, among others—demonstrated the importance of standing up for one's beliefs. He met civil rights leader Dr. Martin Luther King Jr. when he was seventeen years old. "He encouraged us to imagine a better Harlem," he remembered, "and beyond Harlem, a better America." At age twenty, he sat alongside champion heavyweight boxer and lifelong friend Muhammad Ali in public support of Ali's decision not to fight in the controversial Vietnam War.

A private person, Abdul-Jabbar mainly kept to himself during his basketball career. Since his retirement in 1989, however, he has embraced the role of athlete-activist. He has used his platform to speak out and write about racial inequality, religious intolerance, and the need for better education for children. He began supporting cancer research in 2009 after being diagnosed with a form of leukemia. In 2012, as a cultural ambassador of the United States, he brought his plea for improved education to other countries.

President Barack Obama recognized Abdul-Jabbar's lifelong efforts for positive change in 2016 with the Presidential Medal of Freedom and again in 2017, when he appointed him to the President's Council on Sports, Fitness, and Nutrition. "Physically, intellectually, spiritually, Kareem is one of a kind," Obama said at the 2016 medal ceremony. "An American who illuminates both our most basic freedoms and our highest aspirations."

These days, Abdul-Jabbar calls upon other athlete-activists, particularly black athletes, to join him in using their fame to promote awareness of social issues. "They have a responsibility not just to defend a goal or a hoop," he recently wrote, "but also to defend American values and ideals."

RANDY SHILTS

August 8, 1951–February 17, 1994

"Prejudice makes prisoners of both the hated and the hater."

Seventy-eight million people have contracted HIV, or the human immunodeficiency virus—a virus that attacks the human immune system—since 1981. Thirty-five million have died of AIDS, or acquired immunodeficiency syndrome, the name given to the disease whose symptoms are exhibited by late-stage HIV sufferers. Journalist and author Randy Shilts was one of those thirty-five million; before he died, he made sure people did not let the crisis pass in silence.

Shilts was a journalism student at the University of Oregon when he came out as gay. After college, he moved to San Francisco, then the epicenter of America's gay culture. He took a job as a reporter, covering issues facing the gay population, which is how he came to know Harvey Milk. When Milk was assassinated in 1978, Shilts felt compelled to write a book about his life. He interviewed hundreds of people who'd known Milk. Those interviews became the basis for his first book, *The Mayor of Castro Street: The Life and Times of Harvey Milk*. The book caught the attention of the *San Francisco Chronicle*, which offered him a job. He accepted, and in so doing became one of the first openly gay journalists to work for a mainstream newspaper.

Shilts continued to write about topics concerning the gay community. In the early 1980s, one particular topic drew his attention: AIDS, the mysterious illness that seemed to single out gay and bisexual men. After a few years of reporting on the growing epidemic—and on the troubling lack of government action to address it—Shilts turned his research into a book. "I wasn't just an author doing a story," he said at the time. "I live in the gay community and AIDS is a part of my life."

And the Band Played On: Politics, People, and the AIDS Epidemic was published in 1987. Earlier that same year Shilts learned that he, too, had HIV. And yet he didn't disclose his condition until 1993. Why? "Every gay writer who tests positive ends up being an AIDS activist," he once explained. "I wanted to keep on being a reporter."

Shilts did continue to report for the *Chronicle* while battling the disease. He published another book, *Conduct Unbecoming: Gays and Lesbians in the U.S. Military, Vietnam War to the Persian Gulf*. The following February, Shilts passed away. He would not be forgotten, and, thanks to his tireless journalism, neither would the millions of other victims of the HIV/AIDS crisis.

BREAKING NEWS

KAILASH SATYARTHI

January 11, 1954–

"There is no greater violence than to deny the dreams of our children."

Five-year-old Kailash Satyarthi was heading to school one morning when he saw a boy his age working in a cobbler shop. Why was the boy working instead of going to school? Kailash wondered. The answer was simple: the boy's family couldn't afford to send him. Like hundreds of thousands of other children throughout India and the world, he would spend the rest of his days as an uneducated laborer.

That childhood encounter sparked Satyarthi's lifelong activism on behalf of children in crisis. As a young teenager, he raised money for school fees and organized textbook donations so that underprivileged children in his community could get an education. After graduating from college, he took part in raids of factories where children were forced to work. For this, he was badly beaten on more than one occasion.

But Satyarthi refused to back down then—or ever. In 1980, he left a teaching career to create Bachpan Bachao Andolan (Save Childhood Movement), the first-ever foundation in India to fight the exploitation of children. Since its inception, BBA has liberated, educated, and rehabilitated more than 86,000 young victims of slavery, forced military service, and human trafficking. In 1994, he founded GoodWeave International, a nonprofit network of businesses that focuses on ending child labor in the rug-making industry. In 1998, he spearheaded the first Global March Against Child Labour, an international march of concerned groups and citizens that crisscrosses the globe from Southeast Asia to the west coast of South America. And in 2004, Satyarthi started a second worldwide organization, the Kailash Satyarthi Children's Foundation, with the dual mission of promoting education for and ending all forms of violence against children.

For his tireless efforts on behalf of the most vulnerable and powerless members of society, even when his own life was at stake, Satyarthi was awarded the Nobel Peace Prize in 2014. "As a child, I had a vision of tomorrow. A vision of that cobbler boy sitting with me in my classroom," Satyarthi said in his acceptance speech, recalling the long-ago morning. "Now that tomorrow has become today."

LOVE
HUMANITY

WILLIAM HENRY "BILL" GATES

October 28, 1955–

"Being an optimist isn't about knowing that life used to be worse. It's about knowing how life can get better."

In 1968, a scrawny thirteen-year-old math whiz named Bill Gates sat down at a computer terminal for the first time. By the first keystroke, he was hooked. "I wanted to figure out exactly what it could do," he later recalled. He wrote his first program, a tic-tac-toe game, that same year.

The more he learned about computers, the more convinced he became that they would play a key role in humankind's future. By 1975, he had a dream: "A computer on every desktop and in every home." That year, he and his friend Paul Allen founded Microsoft and began developing software for PCs, or personal computers. By 1983, their ingenuity and hard work had turned Microsoft into a multibillion-dollar empire. By 1993, Gates was one of the richest people on the planet.

That's when his mother, Mary Gates, sent him a letter that would steer him in a new direction. "From those to whom much is given," she wrote, "much is expected." Those words struck home for Bill. He realized his wealth put him in a unique position to effect positive change for those less fortunate. In 1994, he began channeling his resources and brainpower into philanthropic causes. Six years later, he and his wife, Melinda, established the Bill & Melinda Gates Foundation.

The foundation is driven by a single overriding motto: All Lives Have Equal Value. Its goal is to empower troubled populations around the globe, including some within the United States, by helping them combat three major problems: disease, poverty, and lack of education. Better health care, more productive and sustainable farming, and access to learning for all are among the foundation's biggest ongoing social programs—a far cry from Gates's first tic-tac-toe computer program.

In 2010, Gates spearheaded a new campaign, the Giving Pledge, with another multibillionaire, Warren Buffett. The Pledge encourages the world's wealthiest people to donate a portion of their fortunes to charity. Gates, Allen, and 173 other billionaires have already signed on. Individually, Gates has given close to $50 billion to other philanthropic causes, and he plans to keep giving.

Once, Bill Gates's belief was in the impact computers would have on humankind. Nowadays? "I'm an optimist about the power of philanthropy," he said. "And so much more is possible."

ANTHONY BOURDAIN

June 25, 1956–June 8, 2018

"Male, female, gay, straight, legal, illegal, country of origin– who cares? You can either cook an omelet or you can't."

Chef and author Anthony Bourdain believed that food had the power to unite. "Walk in someone else's shoes," he once quipped. "Or at least eat their food. It's a plus for everybody."

Bourdain knew he wanted to sample the foods of the world when, as a young child traveling with his family in France, he tasted his first oyster. Throughout college, he worked in restaurants, eventually enrolling in the Culinary Institute of America in New York. After graduating in 1978, he worked for twenty years at top restaurants in Manhattan. A natural storyteller with biting wit, Bourdain chronicled his restaurant kitchen experiences in a bestselling book, *Kitchen Confidential: Adventures in the Culinary Underbelly.*

The book's success opened doors for Bourdain. In 2000, he began a months-long world tour of the world, eating his way through Morocco, Russia, Mexico, and more. He turned his travels into his second bestseller, *A Cook's Tour: In Search of the Perfect Meal*, and a television series by the same name. Bourdain's openness to new experiences made the show a success.

Bourdain stood apart from many other people, both in the food industry and not, due to his willingness to speak out about difficult truths and listen to the less powerful. He was always learning and proud of it. Traveling the world for his long-running series, *Anthony Bourdain: Parts Unknown*, he did not tell people how to cook; he listened to their stories, rejoiced in their expertise, and shared their tables. He was also open about his struggle in recovering from drug and alcohol addictions, and discussed his concerns that he had contributed to a toxic culinary culture when he was younger. He strove to do better. When other famous male chefs were accused of predatory behavior, Bourdain stood with the women accusing them.

In 2018, people around the world were stunned when Bourdain died by suicide, not having known that he was struggling. They began talking about the importance of reaching out to each other, about the pain of addiction and illness. Flowers and notes thanking Bourdain covered the front of his restaurant. "He taught us about food," President Barack Obama wrote. "But more importantly, about its ability to bring us together. To make us a little less afraid of the unknown. We'll miss him."

JOHN BENNETT HERRINGTON

September 14, 1958–

"Those opportunities that come along in your life, take advantage of them, because you only have one shot at it."

John Bennett Herrington made history on November 23, 2002, when he blasted off into outer space aboard the shuttle *Endeavour*, and again a few days later, when he stepped out of the International Space Station for his first space walk. He was the first tribally enrolled Native American to go to space. He carried the Chickasaw Nation's flag, six eagle feathers, a wooden flute, and two arrowheads.

"Flying in space is an incredible experience," he said. "It's just a remarkable adventure."

That remarkable adventure began in his childhood. Like many children raised in the 1960s, he was spellbound by the world's first astronauts and their missions in space. "I used to sit in a cardboard box and dream I was going to the moon," he recalled.

To follow in his heroes' footsteps, he needed to get a solid education in STEM. He struggled at first—after two years, he dropped out of college. But with encouragement and mentorship from people who saw promise in him, Herrington returned to school and earned a bachelor's degree in applied mathematics. He went on to become an aviator for the navy, logging 3,800 hours of flight time aboard more than thirty different aircraft, and getting a master's degree in aeronautical engineering.

In 1996, Herrington was selected by NASA—National Aeronautics and Space Administration—for its space program. He trained for two years, then became a member of the space shuttle pre-launch preparation and post-mission landing operations. Finally, he took his historic 2002 mission into outer space.

Herrington retired from NASA in 2005. Since then, he has pursued a new mission: to introduce and encourage STEM education in schools around the country. He raised the profile of his campaign in 2008 by pairing it with a four-month, 4,000-mile coast-to-coast bike ride he called Rocketrek. He was particularly keen to share his experience, knowledge, and insights into STEM with Native students, saying, "This is my way of returning the favor to those who have impacted my life." He is paying the support forward.

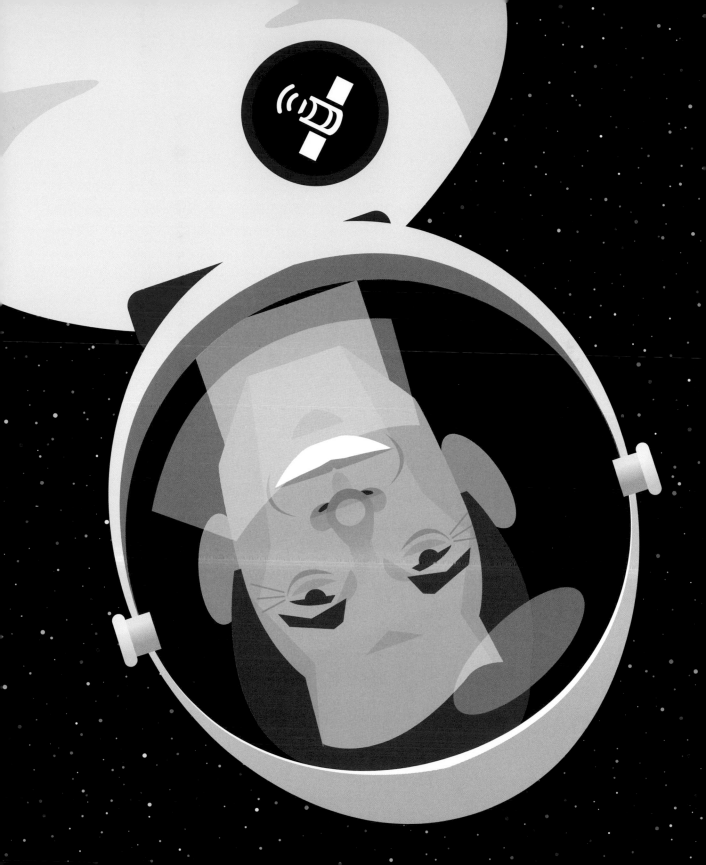

GEORGE CLOONEY

May 6, 1961–

"You never really learn much by hearing yourself speak."

If not for superstar celebrity George Clooney and some of his famous friends, a horrifying humanitarian crisis might have gone unnoticed in the United States. Growing up, Clooney learned a lot about how the news worked from watching his father, the journalist and network anchor Nick Clooney. His family was often very public, and Clooney knew from a young age that the show must always go on. He also knew, from his father's career, that important news events were often overshadowed by celebrity gossip. After years of seeing scary news be ignored in favor of fun news, in 2003, Clooney decided to use his celebrity to bring attention to the important news.

War had broken out in the Darfur region of Sudan, a country in northeast Africa. The Sudanese government began a violent genocide of the Darfuri people that to date has reportedly left 10,000 dead—the actual figure may be in the hundreds of thousands—and millions more homeless and poverty-stricken. Due to racism and international apathy, there was very little coverage of this crisis in the United States. Clooney wanted to change that.

In response to the genocide in Darfur, he and fellow actors Don Cheadle, Brad Pitt, Matt Damon, and more founded Not On Our Watch, a nonprofit whose main goal is to bring attention to international crises. In 2005, Clooney traveled throughout the war-torn Darfur region. A year later, at a rally held on the National Mall in Washington, DC, he spoke about the horrors he'd witnessed. "Every day we don't do something, and every day this goes on," he warned, "thousands of people are dying."

Clooney's humanitarian-aid efforts continue. He was named a United Nations Messenger of Peace in 2008, a position that has allowed him to increase awareness of global crises. In 2009, he donated $1 million to the United Way to help those still living in inadequate conditions in the wake of Hurricane Katrina. In late 2016, he and his wife, Amal, an international human-rights lawyer, established the Clooney Foundation for Justice with the dual goals of combatting injustice and empowering the powerless.

Among the CFJ's biggest projects in 2018 was aid for immigrant children separated from their parents at the United States border. Clooney said, "In the future, our children will ask us: Is it true, did our country really take babies from their parents?" He said that, although he could not change policy, he could and would defend its victims with all the resources at his command.

BARACK HUSSEIN OBAMA

August 4, 1961–

"We are the change that we seek."

At the 2004 Democratic National Convention, an unknown state senator with an uncommon name captivated the audience with a stirring speech about unity, hope, and the need for change. Word quickly spread about the dynamic young politician. Four years later, Barack Obama rode a wave of optimism into the White House as the first African American ever to be elected president of the United States. "If there is anyone out there who still doubts that America is a place where all things are possible," he said in his victory speech, "tonight is your answer."

Obama's rise to the top was meteoric—and merited. The biracial son of a divorced couple, raised by his white grandmother in a predominantly white community in Hawaii, Obama saw better than most the challenges facing marginalized groups. "I stood in front of the mirror," he recalled, "and wondered if something was wrong with me." With his strong empathy, he was able to understand people from different backgrounds and connect with them all.

In college, Obama discovered the power of words and later, in graduate school, so impressed his colleagues with his persuasive arguments that they elected him president of the prestigious *Harvard Law Review*, the first African American to hold that position. He went on to successful careers as a civil rights lawyer, law professor, state senator, and US senator. In each, he championed the embattled rights of children, women, the poor, and people of color, among other causes.

As president, Obama continued his fight for human rights. He implemented DACA (Deferred Action for Childhood Arrivals) to protect the children of illegal immigrants from deportation, and supported legislation to eliminate Don't Ask, Don't Tell—a military policy that barred openly gay, lesbian, and transgender people from serving in the military. He came to champion same-sex marriages, signed the Hate Crimes Prevention Act, and banned the use of torture. He reached out to international communities, too, with the goal of eradicating the threat of nuclear war, which hung over the heads of all people. For this, he was awarded the 2009 Nobel Peace Prize— the first African American man to be so honored since Dr. Martin Luther King Jr. in 1964.

Obama left the White House in January 2017. In his farewell address, he reminded listeners of his strongly held belief: "Change only happens when ordinary people get involved, get engaged, and come together to demand it." And he ended with the three words that had originally launched his campaign, words he still believed and would keep fighting to prove:

"Yes, we can."

YO-YO MA

October 7, 1955–

"Passion is one great force that unleashes creativity."

"**N**ow here's a cultural image for you to ponder as you listen: a seven-year-old Chinese cellist playing old French music for his new American compatriots." This was the introduction conductor Leonard Bernstein gave child prodigy Yo-Yo Ma at a concert in November 1962. It perfectly summed up Ma's international reach, both that night and in the decades-long career that followed.

Born in Paris to musically inclined parents—his mother was a singer and his father a composer and music teacher—Ma began learning the cello when he was just four years old. By age seven, his remarkable talent earned him a spot at Juilliard, one of the world's premier performing arts schools, in New York City. At age sixteen, however, he switched schools to study anthropology at Harvard University. "I needed to grow up someplace," he said of that decision. "I knew I was too young to go out in the world. I knew how little I knew."

It was at Harvard that Ma's interest in other cultures first blended with his love for music. Today, he shares those intertwined passions through the Silk Road Project, an organization he founded in 1998. Named for the historic trade route between Europe and Asia, the Silk Road Project aims to unify diverse cultures by sharing musical traditions, exploring new approaches to music, and exchanging ideas about music's historic impact throughout the globe. "It's a local-global thing," he once explained. "In the cultural world, you want to make sure that voices don't get lost, that fabulously rich traditions live on."

In his ongoing quest to open the world of music to all, Ma has stretched far beyond classical music concerts. The man who has performed for eight presidents, including John F. Kennedy and Barack Obama, has also teamed up with comedian Stephen Colbert, visited with Fred Rogers on *Mister Rogers' Neighborhood*, and played with the Muppets musical group the Three Honkers on *Sesame Street*. He's collaborated with bluegrass, jazz, and Brazilian musicians; filmed a documentary about music with the Bushmen of the Kalahari; and performed with ensembles in shopping malls. On September 11, 2011, he paid moving musical tribute to those who lost their lives in the 9/11 World Trade Center terror attacks.

The winner of sixteen Grammy Awards and the recipient of the 2001 National Medal of Arts and the 2010 Presidential Medal of Freedom, Ma is currently serving as a United Nations Messenger of Peace. But no matter where, what, or for whom he plays, Ma's expressive performances can be summed up with one word: passion.

KYLAR W. BROADUS

August 28, 1963–

"We just want to be ourselves."

Kylar Broadus knew from a very early age that the gender assigned to him wasn't right. He went through his daily activities—school, band, home life—being called a girl while wishing he could be seen differently. But back then, during the 1960s and '70s, very few people acknowledged the existence of transgender people, let alone understood or supported their identities. "I went through years of confusion and unhappiness because who I was told I was didn't fit my own feelings about myself," he once said.

Kylar lived like that until, at age thirty-two, he made the brave choice to come out as a man, knowing the discrimination he would likely face. His employer was not happy with that choice. Broadus suffered months of harassment before being fired—or "constructively discharged," as it was called.

That's when Broadus made another incredible choice: to earn a law degree so that he could file a discrimination lawsuit against the company. He lost the case because Missouri, where he lived, had no laws protecting the rights of those challenging their assigned gender identity.

In response, Broadus began defending people who experienced the same kind of discrimination. He also founded the Trans People of Color Coalition, a national organization combatting the injustices those communities faced. Broadus has also served as a member or director of several national associations for human rights, including the National Black Justice Coalition, the National LGBTQ Task Force, the Human Rights Campaign, and the Transgender Civil Rights Project. Smart, funny, and eloquent, he often speaks to audiences of all kinds about LBGTQ rights and concerns.

His most famous speaking engagement was in 2012, when he became the first openly transgender person to testify before a US Senate committee. He was there to support the Employment Non-Discrimination Act, or ENDA, a proposed law intended to prevent discrimination in employment on the basis of a person's gender identity or sexual orientation. Two years later, he stood proudly alongside other supporters of equality of treatment for LGBTQ persons as President Barack Obama signed an executive order protecting civilian federal employees against discrimination on the basis of gender identity or sexual orientation.

TERRY CREWS

July 30, 1968–

"Vulnerability is not weakness."

Actor, athlete, and activist Terry Crews has worn a lot of hats—and several football helmets. A defensive end on the Western Michigan University football team, he helped the Broncos win the 1988 Mid-American Conference title. The Los Angeles Rams of the NFL drafted him in 1991. He played for the Rams, the San Diego Chargers, the Washington Redskins, and the Philadelphia Eagles, where he ended his football career in 1997.

But Crews had a plan. "I'm going to play NFL," he once told his wife, Rebecca, "and then I'm going to Hollywood to make movies." His charisma, booming voice, and pinpoint comedic timing soon landed Crews roles in commercials, then television shows and movies, including his role as Sergeant Terry Jeffords on the television comedy *Brooklyn Nine-Nine*.

Crews was at the height of success in 2017 when he revealed that in the year before, he had been touched inappropriately by a Hollywood executive. As powerful a figure as he seemed, in the moment that someone touched him without his consent, Crews was powerless—especially because, as a black man, he knew he couldn't seem angry without repercussions that would threaten his career.

He could have stayed silent. He knew that people would judge him or not believe him. Instead he talked, first to the public and then before the Senate Judiciary Committee in support of the Survivors' Bill of Rights Act. "I know how hard it is to come forward," he testified. "I know the shame associated with the assault. I wanted these survivors to know that I believed them… and that this happened to me too."

Crews continues to speak out about masculinity: About growing up with an abusive father and thinking that that was the way men were supposed to be. About wanting to be better for the women in his life. About how the only way that men can do better—can be kind, compassionate people—is by talking to each other about it.

And, thanks to Terry Crews using his big voice, the conversation keeps moving forward.

ZIAUDDIN YOUSAFZAI

December 7, 1969–

"While living in Pakistan, I saw my own shifting ideas to be based more on love, decency, and humanity."

Ziauddin Yousafzai is known to the world as the father of Malala, the Pakistani girl who at age fifteen survived being attacked by the Taliban—a violent fundamentalist group—after she spoke out against their order banning girls from school. Even though he knew the very real dangers facing his daughter, Yousafzai fully supported her defiance. Unlike many men all around the world, he had been a lifelong advocate of women's rights—even when he didn't have to be. "The story of women," he once said, "is the story of injustice, inequality, violence, and exploitation." He wanted to rewrite that story, not just for Malala but for all women, by providing them access to education.

Long before Malala's birth, Yousafzai founded a school that welcomed any girl who wished to attend. He was dedicated to working for peace and equality.

Even after the Taliban tried to assassinate his daughter, Yousafzai remained committed to his cause: supporting not only all women's rights but his daughter's voice and vision, no matter what. In 2013, he and Malala cofounded Malala Fund, which invests in greater access to education for girls and women in areas where women's rights are severely oppressed. Since its founding in 2015, he has served on the board of the Global Peace Centre Canada, or GPCC, a nonprofit organization that promotes education through scholarships, teacher development, and learning resources. Most recently, Yousafzai was appointed a United Nations Special Advisor on Global Education.

Yousafzai's story is the stirring reminder that there are many ways for men to do good in this world, and one of them is by simply lifting up the voices of others. Yousafzai educated, defended, and championed his daughter, making it possible for her to become an internationally recognized icon. He knew that if his daughter was smart, strong, and vocal, it would be a better world for everyone—and he could help her get there. "Education is the only way for the emancipation of women," he once said. "It's their way to independence…to their life as a human being."

QUESTLOVE

January 20, 1971–

"Decide who you're not before you decide who you are."

Ahmir Khalib Thompson, better known as Questlove, is the drummer for the Roots, a ground-breaking hip-hop group from Philadelphia that is now the house band for *The Tonight Show Starring Jimmy Fallon*. While he is a superb percussionist, he was not content to stop there. The multi-instrumentalist, bestselling author, deejay, and social media guru is also a champion of several philanthropic campaigns to help underserved children.

He became part of one such cause in 2010 after seeing *Waiting for Superman*, a documentary film revealing significant failures in public education. Despite his own access to better schools, Questlove felt a connection with the students profiled in the film, because during his teenage years, the threat of falling behind and ending up in a school that didn't care about his future had always hung over his own head.

Questlove reached out to the Harlem Village Academies, a progressive charter school system. He met with aspiring young musicians and raised funds for the school through benefit concerts and creative ventures like the "Questlove Roll," a Philly cheesesteak–Japanese sushi combination.

Questlove has helped children more directly, too. In 1997, he returned home from a tour to discover some young boys sleeping in his Philadelphia house. When his house sitter explained that they had nowhere else to go, Questlove let the boys stay, and wrote each of them letters of recommendation so that they could attend safer schools. Not only did he keep in touch with them, but some of those kids are now adults who work for him as producers.

More recently, Questlove took a role on the advisory board of Edible Schoolyard NYC, a group that teaches young people how to garden and cultivate healthy eating habits. And through his music, his public writing, and his social media posts, Questlove is an outspoken voice against discrimination. "Peaceful protesting is just about the most considerate thing one can do when those in power refuse to listen/believe/acknowledge pain," he once tweeted.

LIN-MANUEL MIRANDA

January 16, 1980–

"You are perfectly cast in your life.
I can't imagine anyone but you in the role. Go play."

In 2015, the multitalented singer-songwriter, rapper, actor, author, and director Lin-Manuel Miranda took the world by storm with his Broadway smash hit *Hamilton*. The musical told the story of Caribbean immigrant and American Revolutionary War hero Alexander Hamilton with an utterly unique blend of musical genres and actors of color playing America's founders. "Our cast looks like America looks now," Miranda said of his groundbreaking casting decision. Miranda, who is Puerto Rican and spent a month every year of his childhood on the island, played the title role.

With his breakout fame after the success of *Hamilton*, Miranda did something unexpected: he was kind. He became known for his warm, generous spirit as much as for his brilliant, radical writing. On Twitter, in the free street shows outside *Hamilton*'s theater, and in his writing, he relentlessly fosters inclusion and empathy, telling everyone that they matter and can make a difference.

In March 2016, Miranda and a few cast members performed at the White House for President Obama, First Lady Michelle Obama, and others. A day later, he took on a different role: activist. That afternoon, he stood with members of Congress in support of a bill to ease Puerto Rico's growing debt crisis, which was causing enormous financial problems for island residents. "I have a lot of family who are struggling in Puerto Rico," he said. "That's not an abstract issue for me."

Little more than a year later, Miranda took further action to help Puerto Rico. In mid-September 2017, the island was devastated by Hurricane Maria. The aid from relief agencies, including that from the rest of the United States, wasn't nearly enough. To help, Miranda wrote and released a song, "Almost Like Praying," with all proceeds going to the Puerto Rican hurricane disaster relief.

Miranda also announced he would reprise his role as Hamilton with a three-week run of the show in San Juan, Puerto Rico, in January 2019.

Hamilton was not Miranda's first musical: his 2005 Broadway debut was a musical called *In the Heights*, inspired by Miranda's own life and family growing up in New York City, that joyously, proudly celebrates home. Even as Miranda's stage and film career continues to take off, one thing is clear: he never forgets home.

KENDRICK LAMAR

June 17, 1987–

"Nothing really changes until I change myself."

Grammy Award–winning rapper, singer, and songwriter Kendrick Lamar made history in 2018, when his 2017 album *DAMN.* was awarded the Pulitzer Prize for Music. He was the first rapper and the first artist not trained in classical or jazz music to win the award. His songs, the awards committee said, captured "the complexity of modern African American life."

"It's an honor," Lamar said of receiving the award. "Been writing my whole life, so to get this kind of recognition is beautiful."

Lamar grew up in Compton, California, a city famous for its fast-paced, innovative gangsta rap music and infamous for the gang violence of the 1990s. Lamar was no stranger to his hometown's struggles—before his tenth birthday, he had witnessed two murders—but instead of feeling crushed beneath them, he began writing down what he'd seen and how he felt. "We used to wonder what he was doing with all that paper," his father remembered. "I thought he was doing his homework!"

Lamar was churning out brilliant lyrics and music so powerful that by age sixteen, he had his first record deal. His songs deliver strong, heartfelt messages about racism and provoke discussions about racial inequality and violence against African Americans, particularly young men subjected to the violence Lamar had seen growing up, and expected to be nothing but violent themselves. His song "Alright," which he wrote to share hope for change with everyone who needed it, caught on like wildfire. It was nominated for four Grammys, winning two, and its lyrics were chanted at protests in support of the Black Lives Matter movement.

Like many successful artists, Lamar donates broadly to charities, like Habitat for Humanity, and initiatives for social change such as President Obama's My Brother's Keeper and John Legend's Free America and Show Me campaigns. However, Lamar's giving also has an urgent personal drive. Lamar found a way through violence and oppression to make his voice heard. Now he's doing what he can to help others find their way through, too, with generous donations to the Compton Unified School District for their music, arts, sports, and after-school programs.

"Being from the city of Compton and knowing the parks that I played at and neighborhoods," he said, "I always thought how great the opportunity would be to give back to my community."

And he has.

SOURCE NOTES

JOHN STUART MILL

"Bad men need nothing more": John Stuart Mill, *Inaugural Address Delivered to the University of St. Andrews, Feb. 1st, 1867: People's Edition* (London: Longmans, Green, Reader, and Dyer, 1867), 36, https://www.goodreads.com/author/quotes/57651.John_Stuart_Mill.

"tyranny of the majority": John Stuart Mill, *On Liberty*, 2nd ed. (London: John W. Parker and Son, 1859), 13, https://www.iep.utm.edu/milljs/#SH2f.

ROBERT SMALLS

"My race": https://robertsmalls-history-fair.weebly.com/photo-gallery.html.

"Good morning, sir!": Walter Coffey, "Surrendering the C.S.S. *Planter*," *Civil War Months* (blog), May 13, 2017, https://civilwarmonths.com/2017/05/13/surrendering-the-c-s-s-planter/.

LOUIS BRANDEIS

"If we desire": "Justice Louis D. Brandeis," Louis D. Brandeis Legacy Fund for Social Justice (web page), accessed October 8, 2018, https://www.brandeis.edu/legacyfund/bio.html.

"right to be let alone": Samuel D. Warren and Louis D. Brandeis, "The Right to Privacy," *Harvard Law Review* 4, no. 5 (December 15, 1890), http://faculty.uml.edu/sgallagher/Brandeisprivacy.htm.

DALIP SINGH SAUND

"I don't care": Bina Murarka, "Dalip Singh Saund—Member of the US House of Representatives," *India West*, August 1, 1977 (updated May 14, 2014), http://www.indiawest.com/online_features/dalip-singh-saund---member-of-u-s-house/article_f095e7c4-dbb6-11e3-9c77-0019bb2963f4.html.

"Ten years ago": Pieter Friedrich, "First Asian in US Congress Was a Sikh Inspired by Civil Rights Principles," *India West*, August 5, 2015, http://www.indiawest.com/blogs/first-asian-in-u-s-congress-was-a-sikh-inspired/article_1f76fde2-3b71-11e5-ac41-1bafc2ce7063.html.

"We have been coddling": "Dalip Singh, Saund (Judge)," History, Art & Archives, United States House of Representatives (web page), accessed October 8, 2018, http://history.house.gov/People/detail/21228.

FENG-SHAN HO

"Seeing the Jews so doomed": Wayne Chang, "Ho Feng Shan: The 'Chinese Schindler' Who Saved Thousands of Jews," CNN.com (website), updated July 24, 2015, https://www.cnn.com/2015/07/19/asia/china-jews -schindler-ho-feng-shan/index.html.

"I was often asked": Manli Ho, "Remembering My Father, Dr. Feng Shan Ho," *China Daily*, updated September 26, 2007, http://www.chinadaily.com.cn/opinion/2007-09/26/content_6134850.htm.

ALAN TURING

"Sometimes it is the people": "Alan Turing Quotes and Sayings," Inspiring Quotes (website), accessed October 8, 2018, https://www.inspiringquotes.us/author/1651-alan-turing.

JONAS SALK

"Hope lies in dreams": "History of Salk: About Jonas Salk," Salk.edu (website), accessed October 8, 2018, https://www.salk.edu/about/history-of-salk/jonas-salk/.

"Could you patent the sun": Carole Bos, "Jonas Salk—'Could You Patent the Sun?'" AwesomeStories.com (website), October 7, 2013, https://www.awesomestories.com/asset/view/Jonas-Salk-Could-You-Patent-the -Sun-.

"We cannot be certain": "History of Salk," Salk.edu (website), accessed October 8, 2018, https://www.salk .edu/about/history-of-salk/.

JAMES BALDWIN

"Not everything that is faced": James Baldwin, "As Much Truth As One Can Bear" in *The New York Times Book Review*, ed. Randall Kenan, republished in *The Cross of Redemption: Uncollected Writings* (New York: Vintage Books, 2011).

Info about the play and song: "David Baldwin Remembers P.S. 24 School," Vimeo.com (website), accessed October 8, 2018, https://vimeo.com/102143825.

"If I hadn't written that book": James Baldwin, "James Baldwin: The Last Interviews," *The Village Voice*, February 24, 2017, https://www.villagevoice.com/2017/02/24/james-baldwin-the-last-interviews/.

"Your family": Bruce G. Kauffmann, "James Baldwin and The Fire Next Time," HistoryLessons.net, November 30, 2016, https://historylessons.net/james-baldwin-and-the-fire-next-time.

THÍCH NHẤT HẠNH

"Our own life": Thích Nhất Hạnh, *The World We Have: A Buddhist Approach to Peace and Ecology* (Berkeley, CA: Parallax Press, 2008), vii, https://www.goodreads.com/quotes/39624-our-own-life-has-to-be-our-message.

"His ideas for peace": Martin Luther King Jr., Nomination of Thich Nhat Hanh for the Nobel Peace Prize, January 25, 1967, http://www.hartford-hwp.com/archives/45a/025.html.

"A smile": "Thich Nhat Hanh," Plum Village (website), accessed October 9, 2018, https://plumvillage.org/about/thich-nhat-hanh/.

Other sources: "Oprah Talks to Thich Nhat Hanh," Oprah.com (website), accessed October 9, 2018, http://www.oprah.com/spirit/oprah-talks-to-thich-nhat-hanh/2.

CESAR CHAVEZ

"Ours is a revolution of the mind and heart": Cesar Chavez, "Education of the Heart: Cesar Chavez in His Own Words," UFW.org (website), accessed October 9, 2018, https://ufw.org/research/history/education-heart-cesar-chavez-words/.

"Generation after generation": Roger Bruns, *Cesar Chavez: A Biography* (Westport, CT: Greenwood Press, 2005), 19.

"Systemic poisoning": Cesar Chavez, "Cesar Chavez's First Major Address after His 36-day 1988 Fast over the Pesticide Poisoning of Farm Workers," UFW.org (website), accessed October 9, 2018, https://ufw.org/research/history/cesar-chavezs-first-major-address-36-day-1988-fast-pesticide-poisoning-farm-workers/.

FRED ROGER3

"It takes strength": *The World According to Mister Rogers* (New York: Hyperion, 2003), 15.

"I give an expression of care": "Mr. Fred Rogers, Senate Statement on PBS Funding, Delivered May 1, 1969," http://www.americanrhetoric.com/speeches/fredrogerssenatetestimonypbs.htm.

MAURICE SENDAK

"Let the wild rumpus start!": Maurice Sendak, *Where the Wild Things Are* (New York: Harper and Row, 1963, repr. 1991), 25.

"We're animals": "Maurice Sendak: 'Where the Wild Things Are,'" PBS.org (website), accessed October 9, 2018, http://www.pbs.org/now/arts/sendak.html.

HARVEY MILK

"We will not win our rights": "The Official Harvey Milk Biography," MilkFoundation.org (website), accessed October 9, 2018, http://milkfoundation.org/about/harvey-milk-biography/.

"This one has teeth": Les Ledbetter, "Bill on Homosexual Rights Advances in San Francisco," *New York Times*, March 22, 1978, https://www.nytimes.com/1978/03/22/archives/bill-on-homosexual-rights-advances-in-san -francisco.html.

"You gotta give 'em hope": Barack Obama, "Remarks on Presenting the Presidential Medal of Freedom," August 12, 2009, Gerhard Peters and John T. Woolley, eds., The American Presidency Project (website), http://www.presidency.ucsb.edu/ws/index.php?pid=86531.

ROBERTO CLEMENTE

"I want to be remembered": "Roberto Clemente Quotes," BrainyQuote.com (website), accessed October 9, 2018, https://www.brainyquote.com/authors/roberto_clemente.

"What we needed": "Beyond Baseball: The Life of Roberto Clemente," Smithsonian Institution Traveling Exhibition Service (website), http://www.robertoclemente.si.edu/english/virtual_legacy.htm.

"I believe": Ibid.

N. SCOTT MOMADAY

"A word has power": N. Scott Momaday, *The Way to Rainy Mountain* (Albuquerque: University of New Mexico Press, 1969), 33.

"Pan-Indian experience": "N. Scott Momaday: Keeper of the Flame," New Perspectives on the West, PBS.org (website), accessed October 9, 2018, http://www.pbs.org/weta/thewest/program/producers/momaday.htm.

"I am lucky": "N. Scott Momaday, Ph.D., Interview," Academy of Achievement (website), June 28, 1996, updated July 17, 2018, accessed October 9, 2018, http://www.achievement.org/achiever/n-scott-momaday -ph-d/#interview.

"for his writings": "N. Scott Momaday, Ph.D." Academy of Achievement (website), June 28, 1996, updated July 17, 2018, accessed January 8, 2018, http://www.achievement.org/achiever/n-scott-momaday-ph-d/.

WALTER DEAN MYERS

"Reading pushed me": Walter Dean Myers, "About Walter Dean Myers," WalterDeanMyers.net (website), accessed October 10, 2018, http://walterdeanmyers.net/about/.

"She tore it up": "Walter Dean Myers Biography," *Encyclopedia of World Biography* (website), accessed October 10, 2018, http://www.notablebiographies.com/news/Li-Ou/Myers-Walter-Dean.html.

"If we continue": Dashka Slater, "Walter Dean Myers: Storytelling for Those Whose Stories Were Left Off the Shelf," in "The Lives They Lived: Remembering Some of Those We Lost This Year," *New York Times*, December 25, 2014, https://www.nytimes.com/interactive/2014/12/25/magazine/2014-the-lives-they-lived.html.

PATRICK STEWART AND IAN MCKELLEN

"Violence is a choice": Patrick Stewart, "Patrick Stewart: The Legacy of Domestic Violence," *Guardian*, November 26, 2009, https://www.theguardian.com/society/2009/nov/27/patrick-stewart-domestic-violence.

"I've never met a gay person": Hilary Hanson, "Ian McKellen: 'I've Never Met a Gay Person Who Regretted Coming Out,'" HuffingtonPost.com (website), January 27, 2018, https://www.huffingtonpost.com/entry/ian-mckellen-coming-out-no-regret_us_5a6cc5d4e4b0ddb658c6eaee.

"Ian and I would talk for hours": Meg Grant, "Patrick Stewart Finds Light in the Darkness," *AARP: The Magazine*, April/May 2014, https://www.aarp.org/entertainment/style-trends/info-2014/patrick-stewart-aarp-magazine.html.

"Though not able": Marianne Schnall, "Exclusive: Patrick Stewart Calls on Men to End Violence Against Women," HuffingtonPost.com (website), March 19, 2013, updated December 6, 2017, https://www.huffingtonpost.com/marianne-schnall/exclusive-interview-with-_11_b_2900041.html.

"Nothing in life": "Ian McKellen," Stonewall.org.uk (website), accessed October 10, 2018, https://www.stonewall.org.uk/people/ian-mckellen.

MUHAMMAD YUNUS

"Poverty is a threat to peace": Muhammad Yunus, "Nobel Lecture" (delivered in Oslo, December 10, 2006), https://www.nobelprize.org/nobel_prizes/peace/laureates/2006/yunus-lecture-en.html.

"What is the point": Ole Danbolt Mjøs, "Award Ceremony Speech" (delivered in Oslo, December 10, 2006), https://www.nobelprize.org/nobel_prizes/peace/laureates/2006/presentation-speech.html.

"Poverty does not belong": Muhammad Yunus, *Banker to the Poor: Micro-Lending and the Battle Against World Poverty* (New York: Public Affairs, 2007), 259.

CARLOS SLIM HELÚ

"You will make": Carlos Slim Helú, "Letter to Young People," June 1994, http://www.carlosslim.com/carta_ing.html.

"Businessmen": Carlos Slim Helú, "Information, Interviews, Questions and Answers," accessed October 10, 2018, http://www.carlosslim.com/38_ing.html.

"Most people try": Dan Western, "45 Carlos Slim Helu Quotes About Wealth & Success," WealthyGorilla.com (website), accessed October 10, 2018, https://wealthygorilla.com/carlos-slim-helu-quotes/ (and other sources).

HAYAO MIYAZAKI

"You must see with eyes unclouded by hate": Hayao Miyazaki, "See with Eyes Unclouded by Hate," YouTube .com (website), posted February 16, 2016, https://www.youtube.com/watch?v=EISWfdFNiUU.

"I yearned for an earnest and pure world": Robbie Collin, "Hayao Miyazaki Interview: 'I Think the Peaceful Time That We Are Living in Is Coming to an End,'" *Telegraph*, May 9, 2014, https://www.telegraph.co.uk/culture /film/10816014/Hayao-Miyazaki-interview-I-think-the-peaceful-time-that-we-are-living-in-is-coming-to-an -end.html.

MUHAMMAD ALI

"If my mind can conceive it": Muhammad Ali, "If my mind can conceive it, and my heart can believe it," @MuhammadAli, May 11, 2015 at 10:30 a.m., https://twitter.com/muhammadali/status /597785792539308032.

"Man, I ain't got no quarrel": Jon Saraceno, "Appreciation: Muhammad Ali Was a Hero in and out of the Ring," *USA Today*, June 4, 2016, https://www.usatoday.com/story/sports/boxing/2016/06/04/muhammad-ali -appreciation/1635243/.

"a fierce fighter": George Bush, "Statement by President George W. Bush on the Passing of Muhammad Ali," George W. Bush Presidential Center, June 4, 2016, https://www.bushcenter.org/about-the-center /newsroom/press-releases/2016/06/statement-muhammad-ali.html.

BOB ROSS

"Anybody can paint": At around 1:10 on "Bob Ross Painting Happy Trees," YouTube.com (website), posted December 4, 2013, https://www.youtube.com/watch?v=B5Wo1ubuzAE.

"I was the guy": Linda Shrieves, "Bob Ross Uses His Brush to Spread Paint and Joy," *Orlando Sentinel*, July 7, 1990, http://articles.orlandosentinel.com/1990-07-07/lifestyle/9007060122_1_bob-ross-joy-of-painting-pbs/2.

STEVEN SPIELBERG

"I don't dream": Cyrus (contributor), "Top 15 Inspiring Steven Spielberg Quotes," Goalcast.com (website), May 23, 2016, https://www.goalcast.com/2016/05/23/top-15-inspiring-steven-spielberg-quotes/.

"I was a nerd": *60 Minutes*, "Steven Spielberg: A Director's Life Reflected in Film," CBS.com (website), January 10, 2013, https://www.cbsnews.com/news/spielberg-a-directors-life-reflected-in-film/2/.

"I often told people": Ibid.

"Students connect": "USC Shoah Foundation Founder Steven Spielberg Announces IWitness Video Challenge," USC Shoah Foundation (website), February 27, 2013, https://sfi.usc.edu/news/2013/02/usc -shoah-foundation-founder-steven-spielberg-announces-iwitness-video-challenge.

"What would drive a man": Joseph McBride, *Steven Spielberg: A Biography* (New York: Simon & Schuster, 1997), 424.

FREDDIE MERCURY

"I won't be a rock star": "Freddy Mercury, Quotes," Goodreads.com (website), accessed October 10, 2018, https://www.goodreads.com/quotes/199679-i-won-t-be-a-rock-star-i-will-be-a.

"I hope": "Queen Star Dies after AIDS Statement," *Guardian*, November 25, 1991, https://www.theguardian .com/century/1990-1999/Story/0,112639,00.html.

"I'm one of those people": Caroline Coon, "'I Can Dream Up All Kinds of Things'—A Classic Freddie Mercury Interview from the Vaults," *Guardian*, November 22, 2011, https://www.theguardian.com/music/2011 /nov/22/freddie-mercury-interview-rocks-backpages.

"It's to tell everybody": "The Freddie Mercury Tribute Concert," UltimateQueen.co.uk (website), last modified November 25, 2017, http://www.ultimatequeen.co.uk/queen/videos/the-freddie-mercury-tribute-concert.htm.

KAREEM ABDUL-JABBAR

"I can do more than stuff a ball through a hoop": http://skyhookfoundation.org/.

"He encouraged us": Kareem Abdul-Jabbar, "My Personal Story about Martin Luther King, Jr.," KareemAbdulJabbar.com (website), accessed October 10, 2018, https://kareemabduljabbar.com/my -heroes/mlk/.

"Physically, intellectually, spiritually": "Kareem Abdul-Jabbar Gets Medal of Freedom at White House," UCLA Newsroom (website), November 22, 2016, http://newsroom.ucla.edu/stories/kareem-abdul-jabbar-gets -medal-of-freedom-at-white-house.

"They have a responsibility not just to defend a goal or a hoop": Kareem Abdul-Jabbar, "Kareem Abdul-Jabbar: Colin Kaepernick Is a Hero Muhammad Ali Would Be Proud Of," *Sports Illustrated*, December 6, 2017, https://www.si.com/sportsperson/2017/12/06/kareem-abdul-jabbar-colin-kaepernick-si-muhammad-ali-legacy-award.

RANDY SHILTS

"Prejudice makes prisoners": Randy Shilts, *And the Band Played On* (New York: St. Martin's Press, 1987), 408.

"I wasn't just an author": Bob Sipchen, "The AIDS Chronicles: Randy Shilts Writes the Biography of an Epidemic and Finds More Bunglers Than Heroes," *Los Angeles Times*, October 9, 1987, http://articles.latimes.com/1987-10-09/news/vw-8502_1_randy-shilts/2.

"Every gay writer who tests positive": Johnny Miller, "Reporter Randy Shilts Announces He Has AIDS, 1994," *San Francisco Chronicle*, February 7, 2018, https://www.sfchronicle.com/entertainment/article/Reporter-Randy-Shilts-announces-he-has-AIDS-1993-12559020.php.

KAILASH SATYARTHI

"There is no greater violence": Kailash Satyarthi, "Kailash Satyarthi—Nobel Lecture," 2014. https://www.nobelprize.org/nobel_prizes/peace/laureates/2014/satyarthi-lecture_en.html.

"As a child": Ibid.

WILLIAM HENRY "BILL" GATES

"Being an optimist": Bill and Melinda Gates, "The Toughest Questions We Get: Annual Letter 2018," GatesNotes.com (website), February 13, 2018, https://www.gatesnotes.com/2018-Annual-Letter?WT.mc_id=02_13_2018_02_AnnualLetter2018_DO-COM_&WT.tsrc=DOCOM.

"I wanted to figure out exactly what it could do": James Wallace and Jim Erickson, *Hard Drive: Bill Gates and the Making of the Microsoft Empire* (New York: John Wiley & Sons, Inc., 1992), 22.

"A computer on every desktop and in every home": Bill Gates, "About Bill," GatesNotes.com (website), accessed October 10, 2018, https://www.gatesnotes.com/bio.

"From those to whom much is given, much is expected": Madeline Stone, "It Was Bill Gates' Mother Who Pushed Him into Philanthropy after He Became a Billionaire," *Business Insider*, May 10, 2015, http://www.businessinsider.com/bill-gates-mother-inspired-philanthropy-2015-5.

"I'm an optimist": Bill Gates, "The Power of Giving: Philanthropy's Impact on American Life" (speech delivered at the National Museum of American History, Washington, DC, December 1, 2015), https://www .gatesfoundation.org/Media-Center/Speeches/2017/06/Bill-Gates-The-Power-of-Giving-Philanthropys -Impact-on-American-Life.

ANTHONY BOURDAIN

"Male, female": Michael Ruhlman, "So You Wanna Be a Chef—by Bourdain," Ruhlman.com (website), September 20, 2010, http://ruhlman.com/2010/09/so-you-wanna-be-a-chef%E2%80%94-by-bourdain-2/.

"Walk in someone else's shoes": Wil Fulton, "Anthony Bourdain's 23 Essential Quotes on Food, Traveling, and Life," Thrillist.com (website), updated on June 8, 2018, https://www.thrillist.com/culture/the-17-best -anthony-bourdain-quotes#.

"He taught us about food": Barack Obama, "Low plastic stool, cheap but delicious noodles, cold Hanoi beer," @BarackObama, June 8, 2018, https://twitter.com/barackobama/status/1005117568913412098.

JOHN BENNETT HERRINGTON

"Those opportunities": Cindy Chan, "U.S. Astronaut Hopes to Inspire Canadian Youth at Aboriginal Symposium," Epoch Times, December 8, 2009, updated December 16, 2009, https://www.theepochtimes .com/us-astronaut-hopes-to-inspire-canadian-youth-at-aboriginal-symposium_1519663.html.

"Flying in space": "John Herrington: I Dreamed of Being an Astronaut," Profiles of a Nation, Chickasaw.tv (website), accessed October 10, 2018, https://www.chickasaw.tv/videos/john-herrington-profiles-of-a -nation-part-2.

"I used to sit in a cardboard box": John Herrington, "One Hundred Years Hence," University of Idaho News (website), Spring 2017, https://www.uidaho.edu/news/here-we-have-idaho-magazine/past-issues/2017 -spring/john-herrington.

Additional info: "John Bennett Herrington: Biographical Data," NASA.gov (website), August 2005, https:// www.jsc.nasa.gov/Bios/htmlbios/herringt.html.

"This is my way": John Bennett Herrington, "One Hundred Years Hence," https://www.uidaho.edu/news/here -we-have-idaho-magazine/past-issues/2017-spring/john-herrington (embedded video, around minute .50).

GEORGE CLOONEY

"You never really": Cyrus (contributor), "Top 12 Most Inspiring George Clooney Quotes," Goalcast.com (website), November 2, 2016, https://www.goalcast.com/2016/11/02/top-12-inspiring-george-clooney-quotes/.

"Every day we don't": ABC News, "George Clooney Speaks About Crisis in Darfur," ABCNews.go.com (website), April 30, 2006, https://abcnews.go.com/ThisWeek/story?id=1907005.

"In the future": Young Center for Immigrant Children's Rights, "George and Amal Clooney and the Clooney Foundation for Justice Support the Young Center for Immigrant Children's Rights," Press Release, June 20, 2018, https://cfj.org/wp-content/uploads/2017/01/PRESS-RELEASE_Clooney-Foundation-and-Young -Center_2018-06-20.pdf.

BARACK HUSSEIN OBAMA

"We are the change that we seek": Barack Obama, "Barack Obama's Feb. 5 Speech," *New York Times*, February 5, 2008, https://www.nytimes.com/2008/02/05/us/politics/05text-obama.html.

"If there is anyone out there": Barack Obama, "Sen. Barack Obama's Acceptance Speech in Chicago, Ill.," *Washington Post*, November 5, 2008, http://www.washingtonpost.com/wp-dyn/content/article/2008/11/05 /AR2008110500013.html.

"I stood in front of the mirror": Biography.com Editors, "Barack Obama Biography," Biography.com (website), April 2, 2014, updated July 18, 2018, https://www.biography.com/people/barack-obama-12782369.

"Change only happens": Barack Obama, "Read the Full Transcript of President Obama's Farewell Speech," *Los Angeles Times*, January 10, 2017, http://www.latimes.com/politics/la-pol-obama-farewell-speech-transcript -20170110-story.html.

"Yes, we can.": Barack Obama, "Transcript of Barack Obama's Acceptance Speech," NPR.org (website), November 5, 2008, https://www.npr.org/templates/story/story.php?storyId=96624326.

YO-YO MA

"Passion is one great force": Wei-Huan Chen, "Reading between the Notes: The Genius of Yo-Yo Ma," *Journal & Courier*, October 8, 2014, https://www.jconline.com/story/entertainment/music/2014/10/08/yo-yo-ma -purdue/16917373/.

"Now here's a cultural image": Peter B. Kaufman, "Leonard Bernstein Introduces 7-Year-Old Yo-Yo Ma: Watch the Youngster Perform for John F. Kennedy (1962)," OpenCulture.com (website), March 8, 2017, http:// www.openculture.com/2017/03/leonard-bernstein-introduces-7-year-old-yo-yo-ma.html.

"I needed to grow up someplace": Alison Beard, "Life's Work: An Interview with Yo-Yo Ma," *Harvard Business Review* (June 2016), https://hbr.org/2016/06/yo-yo-ma.

"It's a local-global thing": Janet Tassel, "Yo-Yo Ma's Journeys," *Harvard Magazine*, March 1, 2000, https:// harvardmagazine.com/2000/03/yo-yo-mas-journeys-html.

KYLAR W. BROADUS

"We just want to be ourselves": David-Elijah Nahmod, "Meet Kylar W. Broadus," EchoMag.com (website), March 20, 2016, https://echomag.com/kylarwbroadus/.

"I went through years of confusion": Lester Strong, "Kylar Broadus: Advocate," *A&U: America's AIDS Magazine*, May 16, 2016, http://aumag.org/2016/05/16/kylar-broadus-advocate/.

TERRY CREWS

"Vulnerability is not weakness": Tim Ferriss, "How to Have, Be, Do All You Want (#287)," *The Tim Ferriss Show* (blog), December 20, 2017, https://tim.blog/2017/12/20/terry-crews-how-to-have-do-and-be-all-you-want/.

"I'm going to play NFL": Diana Saenger, "Terry Crews: From Football to Filmmaking," Reel Talk Movie Reviews (website), accessed October 11, 2018, http://www.reeltalkreviews.com/browse/viewitem .asp?type=feature&id=181.

"I know how hard it is": Mahita Gajanan, "'This Happened to Me Too': Terry Crews Details His Alleged Sexual Assault During Emotional Senate Testimony," *Time*, June 26, 2018, http://time.com/5322629/terry-crews -sexual-assault-senate-committee/.

ZIAUDDIN YOUSAFZAI

"While living in Pakistan": Ziauddin Yousafzai, *Let Her Fly: A Father's Journey* (New York: Little, Brown, 2018), 72.

"The story of women": Ziauddin Yousafzai, "My Daughter, Malala," TED.com (website) (March 2014), https:// www.ted.com/talks/ziauddin_yousafzai_my_daughter_malala/transcript.

"Education is the only way": Plan International, "One-on-One with Malala's Father, Ziauddin Yousafzai," PlanCanada.ca (website), accessed October 11, 2018, https://plancanada.ca/one-on-one-with-ziauddin -yousafzai.

QUESTLOVE

"Decide who you're not": Adam Grant, "Questlove Wants You to Start Listening—Really Listening—Again," *Esquire*, March 20, 2018. https://www.esquire.com/entertainment/a19181322/questlove-original-thinkers -april-2018/.

"Peaceful protesting": Katherine Brooks, "Questlove: 'It's a Shame' Celebrities Have to Speak Out When Politicians Don't," HuffingtonPost.com (website), September 26, 2017. https://www.huffingtonpost.com/entry /questlove-its-a-shame-celebrities-have-to-speak-out-when-politicians-dont_us_59c8626fe4b0cdc7733218f5.

LIN-MANUEL MIRANDA

"You are perfectly cast": Lin-Manuel Miranda, "Good morning. You are perfectly cast in your life. I can't imagine anyone but you in the role. Go play," @Lin_Manuel, April 29, 2016, https://twitter.com/lin_manuel /status/726025564696502272.

"Our cast looks like": Michael Paulson, "'Hamilton' Heads to Broadway in a Hip-Hop Retelling," *New York Times*, July 12, 2015, https://www.nytimes.com/2015/07/13/theater/hamilton-heads-to-broadway-in-a-hip -hop-retelling.html.

"I have a lot of family": Carolina Moreno, "Lin-Manuel Miranda: On Why Puerto Rico's Debt Crisis Is a 'Life or Death Issue,'" HuffingtonPost.com (website), June 24, 2015, https://www.huffingtonpost.com/entry/lin -manuel-miranda-on-why-puerto-ricos-debt-crisis-is-a-life-or-death-issue_us_576d7d09e4b017b379f5dd56.

KENDRICK LAMAR

"Nothing really changes": Josh Eells, "The Trials of Kendrick Lamar," *Rolling Stone*, June 22, 2015, https:// www.rollingstone.com/music/music-news/the-trials-of-kendrick-lamar-33057/.

"the complexity of": Pulitzer Prizes, "The 2018 Pulitzer Prize Winner in Music: *DAMN.*, by Kendrick Lamar," Pulitzer.org (website), accessed October 11, 2018, https://www.pulitzer.org/winners/kendrick-lamar.

"It's an honor": Derrick Bryson Taylor, "Kendrick Lamar Humbly Accepts Pulitzer Prize, *New York Post*, May 31, 2018, https://pagesix.com/2018/05/31/kendrick-lamar-humbly-accepts-pulitzer-prize/.

"We used to wonder": Josh Eells, "The Trials of Kendrick Lamar," *Rolling Stone*, June 22, 2015, https://www .rollingstone.com/music/music-news/the-trials-of-kendrick-lamar-33057/.

"Being from the city of Compton": Zach Frydenlund, "The California State Senate Honored Kendrick Lamar with the 'Generational Icon Award,'" Complex.com (website), May 12, 2015, https://www.complex.com /music/2015/05/kendrick-lamar-honored-by-california-state-senate.